# IT'S ALL RELATIVE(s)

## Stories of Family & Friendship

By the:

Writers of the Forest

*[signatures]*

Thank you to our family and friends who have supported us in the publication of our inaugural anthology.

--Writers of the Forest

# It's All Relative(s)
## Copyright © 2018 by the Writers of the Forest

Contributing Authors: Claudia Blanchard, Terry L. Dismore, Barbara Dullaghan, Lorraine Gilmore, Lee Norman Mehler, Diane Pascoe, John Stickney, John Stipa, Suzy Tenenbaum.

Editors: Claudia Blanchard, John Stipa

Cover art: Three Generations on Market by Lee Norman Mehler
Cover design and layout: Betsy Stipa

Disclaimer: Each story contained in this book is based on the contributing author's imagination or recollections of events, related to the best of his or her knowledge. No errors, oversights or harm were intended for any individual, organization or company.

CreateSpace Independent Publishing Platform
North Charleston, SC
October 6, 2018

ISBN-13: 978-1-727-61013-0
ISBN-10: 172761013X

Library of Congress Control Number: 2018911597

# WHO ARE THE WRITERS OF THE FOREST?

Every week we gather, people who have a desire to write and who value one another's friendship and insight.

We write fiction, nonfiction, articles, essays, and poems along with the occasional untethered stream of consciousness. Our format challenges the writer, by way of prompts, to spend twenty minutes, without any prior preparation, developing such pieces. The prompts, or idea kick-starters, are sometimes vague and up to interpretation that, almost without fail, stimulate the creative juices. Think for yourself where your imagination runs after you hear: "the silence woke her..." It is the artistic skill of the writer that then takes you somewhere by crafting words on paper.

We are generous with our help, keenly, but kindly analytical of one another's work, and delivered in the spirit of improving our craft.

Time in our gatherings flies quickly, but there is always the promise of a future meeting to look forward to until we can once again sate our need to write.

From left to right: Suzy Tenenbaum, Lee Mehler, Barbara Dullaghan, John Stipa, Claudia Blanchard, John Stickney, Lorraine Gilmore, Diane Pascoe, Terry L. Dismore

# Table of Contents

# I Come From

## By: Lorraine Gilmore

I'm from hot summer nights
filled with lightening bugs.
The water dripping from a sprinkler
and spikes of grass beneath my bare feet.

Sittin' on the front porch
sippin' a Co-cola
and wishin' for an R.C.

Walks through the cool waters of
Gordon's Creek on a hot summer day
under a blue sky with white puffy clouds.
Coming up the creek bank
to pick ripe, red juicy plums.

Butter beans, field peas and hot buttered cornbread,
fried chicken with rice and gravy
followed up with warm peach cobbler and
tall glasses of iced sweet tea.

I'm from a front porch swing
that moved on creaking chains.
Huddled on the floor by the radio
seeking the Scarlet Pimpernel.

One potato, two potato, three potato, four
as we choose sides for softball.
Swinging ropes and Double Dutch
at recess in the schoolyard.

I'm from spare the rod and spoil the child
as my little legs danced on the kitchen floor
after picking a switch big enough to do the job.

I'm from cardboard fans on wooden sticks
that move the sultry air
My sleepy head on mama's lap
has wet, stringy hair.

# The Awful Truth

## By: John Stickney

My own children are well past of the age of belief in Santa Claus. This took a more than a little of the joy and wonder out of the gift part of Christmas morning. But, as any parent soon realizes, it cuts the gift giving and the post-Christmas bills in half. There is less need to mail that letter to the International Monetary Fund begging for that loan necessary to refinance your debt. Also on the upside, you finally get full credit for the gifts that have been given and received. No more need to assemble a bike or Shera's Invincible Fortress/Dream House at 3:00 am on Christmas Eve and then watch mere hours later some jolly fat guy last seen in the mall get all the credit.

I realize that playing Santa is not the easiest job in the world. Once for work, I went into a warehouse that housed the mall Santa suits in the off-season. Rack after rack of flaccid empty red suits hung above cheap shiny black boots anticipating the seasonal return of that Christmas magic. It was like something out of a film by Federico Fellini. The space also housed the Easter Bunny outfits. I tried on one of the floppy-eared heads. The inside smelled like cheap wine and despair.

At my wife's request, I once played Santa. She was employed as a Children's Librarian in a branch on the east side of Cleveland, Ohio. It was a daytime event, mostly attended by a mix of mothers and wide-eyed young children. I played the role years before padding would not be needed. There I sat, stuffed with pillows, trying to keep my "Ho, Ho, Ho's" suitably non-threatening. Each child had such expectant eyes. If you were really evil, you could create an army out of those expectations. It would be a terrible power in someone's misguided hands.

I am no longer certain when or how I learned the terrible truth about Santa Claus, so, for background, I asked my children. My daughter, then approaching 18 years of age, remembered it as if it were yesterday. She was six years old and sleeping over at her grandmother's house. They were seated on the living room sofa together, dressed in their pjs, sipping cocoa and watching reruns of Lawrence Welk or maybe Wheel of Fortune, these seemed to be the only two programs the tv could receive. Out of the blue, her grandmother, my wife's mother for those like me who think it matters, turned to her and said, "You don't believe in that nonsense about Santa Claus and the Easter Bunny, do you?"

"Grandma," my daughter recalled saying, "not anymore."

"I'm so glad," her grandmother said, "that I don't have to pretend around you. You know your cousin Hank (Hank was all of five years old), he still believes in that nonsense." My daughter could only shake her head in stunned disbelief.

How did my son learn? He was not sure. But there are two logical sources from which he discovered the terrible truth. First, he rode the bus to school. Besides the colorful language, the off-color jokes, the multitude of theories on where babies came from, and the explanation of who and who does not have cooties and the why, Santa Claus had to be at the minimum a seasonal topic of conversation. Second, he had an older sister, an older sister who passed on other bits of forbidden knowledge, such as where babies really came from and the cheat codes for various video games, knowledge learned before its time.

When asked by my children when I learned the awful truth about Santa Claus, I told them that Chico Marx told me. When I was a kid - as I age being a kid means any age between four and thirty – I was watching a Marx Brothers' film on the TV. I think it was "The Big Store", but it may have been another one. In the film Groucho was discussing some kind of legal contract, which he wanted Chico to sign. Groucho said something like, "Of course you know this contract has a sanity clause." Chico said, "Sanity clause? Sanity clause? Ah, you're kidding me boss, everyone knows there is no such thing as Sanity Claus."

In truth, I do not know when or how I learned the awful truth. I have my suspicions. There's a line of suspects, Chico Marx, my two older sisters, five year's worth of school bus riding companions. In my mind they step forward one by one and say "There's no such thing as Santa Claus." It could have been any one of them. They say a hero dies only one death, a coward one thousand times, for Santa Claus and the innocence of youth there's an infinite, never ending number. Whenever I learned the awful truth, from that point on, in the tradition of those omnipotent voice-overs from the TV's "The Wonder Years", I knew the world would never be the same.

# Pink Sneakers

## By: Suzy Tenenbaum

"What's your name again?" Chelsea asks.

"It's Mrs. Tenenbaum, but you can call me Mrs. T."

It's the first day of school and I don't expect my students to remember my name. In fact, I don't expect much of them at all. I've already learned to keep my expectations of new kindergarteners to a minimum because each class is unique and each child is different.

Sometimes the one who is all chatty at the Open House and who brings me a picture and tells me all about how she made the rainbow for me, is the very one whom I need to peel away from mom the very next day, and who refuses to say a word when we go around the circle and tell our name and favorite color. Kids are unpredictable and that fact is predictable to me. What is also predictable is that they make friends in mysterious ways.

At recess, "What's your name again?" is followed up by "Her and I are best friends. We both have pink sneakers!" Then she raises her hand to show me it is intertwined with her classmate's, as they each wobble to lift a pink foot to prove the point. Best friends already after three hours, and Chelsea didn't speak for two of them! But matching sneakers go a long way in feeling connected when you are five.

Sometimes parents would come to me and tell me of friendships their children were developing. "Hillary has the biggest crush on Wyatt," her mom tells me. "He's all she talks about! She says they are going to get married!"

"She must really like him," I reply. "I'm glad she is making friends so easily." Inside my head I'm arguing, "Hillary and Wyatt?!" I've not seen one word pass between them. Nor have I ever seen them choose one another as partners for our bean bag game, or chase one another at the perpetual kid favorite, tag, that fills most of recess. Hearing about this mysterious bonding leads me to think more deeply about kindergarten friendships and beyond.

What makes for a close friend? I hear my mom at 94 lament the loss of close friends, and I see how hard it can be to make new friends as one gets to old, old age. Her friend Lita got in the car the other day after two years of monthly luncheons and said, "So Helen, are you the one who lost a daughter too? I know another one of us ladies in the group did. Was it you?" There it is, reaching out for a connection. Not pink sneakers, but the loss of a daughter.

In kindergarten, I was fascinated watching the bonds of friendship grow and break and in some cases grow and grow. I saw some children make fast friends the first week of school and maintain those friendships for the next five years. When I'd go to 5th grade graduation, I'd see them standing side-by-side, heads practically touching, giggling and seemingly happy to have created a world together. I can easily reach back to a memory of two of these long-time friends in the dramatic play area, each holding a doll they had carefully wrapped in a blanket, and talking about their babies. Almost as easily I can imagine them twenty years in the future doing the same.

It happened that way for me. Betty Lou and I played dolls together and then we each had three real babies. We talk a couple of times a week now about many things: exercise, aging, politics, movies and books, but at the top of our list of favorite conversation topics is still talking about those babies who now range in age from 28 to 34. Yesterday we talked about her middle son's baby, her first grandchild. We talk about our children in honest, unfiltered ways that we probably wouldn't want others to hear.

We've had a very close friendship for 55 years. When we were teens, she slept in my bed with me for several nights after my sister died. I helped her clean out her mom's closet on the evening after her funeral.

I remember the first day I met Betty Lou. I was ten. My parents were talking with the realtor about buying the house across the street from Betty Lou's family. I met her out on the street and she said, "Hey Girlie!" I had never been called girlie before and I was a little put off, but there was a friendly tone to it and I appreciated that she made the first overture. Little did I know she would become one of the most important people in my life.

There is a lesson here: Be mindful of the sneakers you choose and the salutations you call out on the street. They may lead to friendships that last a lifetime.

# Making A Statement

## By: Barbara Dullaghan

She stood proudly, dare I say defiantly, on the rooftop of the tenement building on Jackson Street in the Bronx, striking a pose one might have seen in a magazine. Her right foot resting on a concrete platform, her left on the floor, it looked as if the picture had been taken before she was totally ready, as part of her right hand stuck out of her pocket. If published today, the black and white photo would be labeled as vintage and, with no commentary to accompany it, the image would probably conjure up many interesting stories.

Dressed in a man's brown three-piece suit and tie, her styled hair, unshaven face, and high heels provided hints to her femininity. The material draped on her tall and slender frame helped her appear comfortable in her outfit, although obviously too big on her judging from the abundance of material on her sleeves. The straw hat, tipped cockily to the side, shaded her lovely face. The tobacco pipe added the final touch to her look.

This is a picture of my Great-aunt Helen taken in the

1930's. When I spent time with her as a young child, she was a wife, mother to my cousin Mary, and sister to my grandmother, Elizabeth, roles that were expected in the 1950's. I remember little of her except for her shaking hands, perhaps a sign of Parkinson's, and her kind smile. There is so much of people's lives we are unaware of and, as I age, I wish I knew all the stories of those lives.

I imagine that her life was filled with low expectations regarding her future, yet her strength and intelligence cemented a thoughtful perspective on her life. In this somewhat intimate photo, Helen seems to be playing a role of a tough woman who has to dress like a man to gain attention.

Was she dressed for a costume party? Was it a joke to elicit chuckles from her fourteen brothers and sisters? Or was she hiding a very big secret?

# My Mother Never

## By: Claudia Blanchard

My mother never turned 40.

She never completed her inaugural year as a first-grade teacher.

My mother never attended my Sweet 16 party.

She never helped me select my wedding dress.

My mother slapped me gently when I first menstruated, apparently a ritual at the time.

My mother cried when I insisted, at the age of 5, that when I married she would have to move and leave our home to me and my husband.

My mother often threatened me with, "Claudia, just wait until your father gets home."

My mother once threw a hairbrush at me from across the dining room table.

Her mantra was, "Claudia, I hope you have a daughter just like you."

My mother never told my father how much trouble I caused in school.

She defended me to my teachers and school principal.

My mother never told me that she was dying.

She simply said, "I want you to live with Nana Evelyn."

I replied, "Never."


From the prompt *finish this sentence*: "My mother never . . ."

# A Seat at the Table

## By: Terry L. Dismore

What are the requirements for a seat at the table, when the chairs have been positioned to keep you out or keep you in?

In these turbulent times, alignment, position, interlocking cultures, peace, love, and unity will reign only as each one allows in their hearts. It's the thoughts and actions of a small group of people shedding light on us all.

Look at the chairs from another angle; what an excellent idea to create chairs that allow everyone to sit together harmoniously at the table. Notice the chairs are connected and linked with authoritative dark bold supporting frames. The patterns are shaded in the midst of light and dark colors revealing dynamic combinations of tightly knitted patterns and designs.

The chairs have been positioned to allow everyone to move as a single unit. You can't separate the chairs without damage to the entire configuration. We all must proceed joined, connected or not at all. Where you go, I must go for survival. The **I's** have been eliminated leaving only **we** and **us**.

The creation and struggle of the chairs are the human elements of choice! Who will lead and who will follow? Will we take turns, share, be kind, say thank you and please, which are all concepts learned in kindergarten.

The chairs are assembled calling humanity to order. These inanimate chairs brand creativity, passion, purpose, and destiny for greatness, not destruction. Did you detect the beauty, strength, uniqueness, poetry, and rhythm in the chairs?

The chairs bow down to a higher order. The chairs know they are chairs so why don't you know who you are and what you represent?

Don't give your power to the sticks of wood, but to the structural beauty and creation of the divine in the chairs. A good mindset created, designed, architectural beauty joined together as one.

In the beginning, questions and thoughts sent to the universe without contour or form summon answers. What are the requirements for a seat at the table? Communication, pure hearts, acceptance, understanding and most of all love for one another are a beginning. After all, the higher order of humanity is us.

The chairs call everyone to take a seat at the table and face each other!

Tom Shields (American) Off—Kilter, nd

# Lightning Strikes Twice

## By: Diane Pascoe

"Diane, there's an urgent call from your husband," said the office assistant as she poked her head into the boardroom where I was meeting with the CEO. "He wants you to call him right now!"

*Oh my gosh. What has happened? Has someone been in an accident? Is the house on fire?* I ran to my office, grabbed the phone and called my husband's cell phone.

A familiar voice said, "Hello."

"Honey, what's wrong?" I asked breathlessly. *His answer had better be good to have dragged me out of my meeting.*

"Do you have the extra key for the Suburban with you?" he asked.

"No, why?"

"I'm at the do-it-yourself car wash with the two dogs. I left the keys on the console between the two front seats, then I got out of the Suburban to wash it. Carley walked over to the driver's window to see what I was doing and stepped on the lock button on the driver's armrest! The two dogs are locked inside the truck at the car wash."

*Lordy! Can't we have just one day without doggie drama? My love for dogs and husbands is being tested.*

I wanted to ask my husband what the heck possessed him to leave the keys in the truck, but I decided against it. Timing is everything in a marriage, so I just bit my tongue. I told him that I would drive home to get the extra key and meet him at the car wash. I envisioned impatient drivers waiting to wash their cars, so I hustled out the office door as quickly as possible to drive forty miles back to the house and car wash.

When I arrived at the truck, I could see our black-and-tan dachshund, Carley, standing at the driver's window eagerly wagging her tail. Wyatt, the Labrador retriever, was sprawled on the back seat, sound asleep and snoring. Curiously, I couldn't see Honey anywhere, but then a tall, familiar man emerged from the bar across the street.

"There was nothing I could do hanging around here," my husband said sheepishly, "so I went to the bar and had a beer." He glanced at our truck, which had been parked in the car wash bay for almost an hour. Maybe he was right —the bar was a better place for him to wait for me.

Taking the extra key out of my pocket, I unlocked the truck door. Carley, who was very excited to see a visitor, then peed on the leather driver's seat, leaving a yellow puddle. *Ohmygod, Carley!*

The good news, if you could call it that, was that just as lightning doesn't strike the same place twice, I knew this disaster would never happen again. I was confident that Honey had learned an important lesson about leaving the keys in a vehicle with dogs in it.

I was wrong.

A few years after this catastrophe, Honey was driving to our future neighborhood to check on our new house that was under construction. He stopped at a gas station, then left the dogs in the BMW while he pumped gas. As Carley hopped from the passenger seat to the driver's seat to watch what was going on, she stepped on a button on the center console, locking all the car doors! This was like a rerun of a very bad movie starring Honey and the dogs — once again he had left the keys in the car, but this time I was a few hours away and couldn't bring him the back-up key.

Given his predicament, he had no choice but to tell the gas station attendant about the car that was locked with two dogs inside. The attendant, following gas station policy, called the town's fire department, which sent two fire trucks and ten firefighters to handle this crisis. Hopefully it was a slow day at the fire department.

Upon arrival, the firefighters assessed the situation as Carley happily wagged her tail and barked at them from the front seat. One firefighter suggested using a coat hanger to unlock the car door, a tried-and-true method for breaking into locked cars. But Germans build very secure autos, so that approach was out; obviously BMW car designers never even considered that husbands could leave keys inside cars or that dachshunds could lock car doors.

A growing crowd of onlookers had assembled to view the emergency requiring so many firefighters—the spectators apparently found the situation much more amusing than did my husband.

In desperation, Honey said to the firefighters, "We have to think like Carley. She doesn't follow instructions very well, nor can she read lips, but she loves people and will eventually come to the window to say hello I think."

So, with Honey at one window and the firefighters at the other, they tried to coax Carley to walk across the center console in the hope that one of her tiny paws would once again hit the button and unlock the door. This vaudeville routine continued unsuccessfully for ten minutes until suddenly the little dachshund stepped on the unlock button as she hopped across the console. *Click!* Everyone let out a loud cheer, as though the dachshund had just hit the jackpot on a slot machine.

I am pleased to report that the dogs have not been accidentally locked in the car since the gas station event, because we have made some constructive changes. First, we bought an SUV that has a cipher lock on the door so that it can be opened without a key. Second, Carley is now safely restrained in the back seat, secured by a new doggie seatbelt harness. No hopping around on the car seats, no locking doors with her little wiener dog paws.

And no more doggie drama to deal with—or at least none involving cars.

# The Cottage

## By: Lee Norman Mehler

John Sessions was going home for the first time.

Actually, it was a second home he had never been to before. He was traveling eleven hours from his West Virginia base. Five hundred miles could be either a line on a map or a lifetime away. He had been tempted for many years to go to "The Cottage" as the family referred to it. But he did not attempt the trip until he had gotten his test results. Once time was not an issue. Now time was the only issue. His diagnosis was "not great". The echo of this phrase rang in his head as his father had used it fifty years before.

"Yeah, genetics are crap sometimes," he muttered to no one. He was frantic and calm at the same time.

***

Doctor Mark Case had said "You need to think about your life in a different way now."

"You mean see the people I should have said I am sorry to?" John said.

"Yes, and also to see if you can make small amends for the

indifference that has become your life."

John thought for a moment and said, "Thanks for being my best friend. Thanks for playing this straight with me."

"Well that's a good beginning. Now go create a new and decent end to your story."

John felt he had a purpose for his short time left.

***

He approached the Michigan retreat of the last person on his list. His journey would end here after touching on the lives of others he had all but forgotten: his two cousins in Topeka, his aunt in Cambridge, his niece and nephew in the Twin Cities. All had accepted the short disruptive presence in their usual lives. Each had opened their hearts a tiny bit for the wishes of a dying man. It had been hard and yet it felt right once the awkwardness passed. They all traded stories of the past about friends and relatives that were still here or gone. John had lost track of them because his lifestyle had crowded out the human contacts that real life demanded. He was trying to gather the missing threads of the family quilt that had unraveled through his neglect.

***

John walked the cobblestone path to the worn gray door of the lake house. Cora Alma Sessions had retired to "The

Cottage" in 1991 not thinking she would live to be 93. Life here was simple and basic as expected. Time was frozen in place.

He was greeted out front by a whirl-a-gig carved by his grandfather Samuel. It was a pioneer woman in a bonnet churning butter. The harder the wind from the south blew, the faster the blade turned, increasing the click, click, click of the churn moving up and down.

The house, reclaimed from the carpenter ants and dry rot, was now sheathed in light green vinyl siding. Otherwise it had not changed since it was built in 1951.

The front porch partially protected a hanging swing that had grayed over the years. There were two chalky white rocking chairs with multicolored crocheted pillows made for older backs to lean on while passing the hours on long summer evenings.

He knocked on the door and instantly recognized the deeply wrinkled, tanned face that greeted him. The kind smile was the same. There was the glint in her light blue eyes that belied the years of hard work in the fields beside her husband and the passage of time.

"Hello John. I was expecting you."

"Hello Grandma."

"I'm glad you could make it here before you and I are gone."

"Better late than never," he uttered before he could stop himself.

"I've set you up in the back bedroom where Jimmy used to stay."

James Charles Hastings was his mother's second husband. Grandma Sessions had taken Jimmy under her wing when he lost his job at the mill. He had moved on years ago when he got a break in the new career he wanted. He had not said "thank you" and she had not expected any gratitude. The Sessions' immediate and extended family members were not good about showing appreciation.

John looked around and absorbed the surroundings that somehow felt like home even though he had never been here before.

John stepped across the well-worn threshold. The inside of the home was the link to the past for Cora. For John this was the salve he needed to mend the wounds of his tired past.

His grandmother had one new habit inherited from her daughter: she required her guests take off their shoes once they entered the house. John felt every fiber of the short brown shag carpet and the off-white linoleum that slightly chilled his feet as he passed from room to room.

The knotty yellow pine walls and the furniture had absorbed the slightly acrid and sweet smell of the burning logs from the wood-burning stove. The stove creaked and groaned as it expanded and contracted.

The living room was crowded with an overstuffed sofa covered with a fabric print of regional fish, an antique walnut rocking chair, and a green La-Z-Boy recliner. Off to the side a blue-gray card table displayed a half-finished jigsaw puzzle of a lake, a house from another decade and a large camp fire outside with sparks reaching for the sky. The puzzle would be completed by the next visitors in the cottage.

They moved to the small, u-shaped kitchen where John danced around his grandmother as he helped himself to a beer she offered from the Norge refrigerator. He noticed the primary colors of the magnetized plastic alphabet letters on the white refrigerator door waiting for the next visit by Cora's great granddaughters.

They sat on the back-porch, previously converted to a sun room. They ate a lunch of fresh chicken salad with almonds, grapes and celery on a thick slab of homemade, cracked wheat toast. The bamboo shades were rolled half-way down to keep the sun out of their eyes as they faced the water. Bush Lake was one of hundreds of small bodies of water in the middle of Michigan's vast forests and farmlands. The perimeter of the lake had a gentle, sandy taper for thirty feet which led to a shelf of reeds and grasses until it suddenly dropped off. The fish would congregate in this vegetation and deeper down this slope.

"Tell me why you are here, John?"

"Because my life is suddenly shorter and I need some closure and some meaning."

"Don't you think that's selfish?"

"Yeah, I suppose it is. But maybe I can get some understanding of why I have taken up space in this world. Maybe I can find a little good for me and for the others I have not spoken to for too long."

Cora hesitated. "This family has been fractured by time and circumstances. Bad choices, bad marriages, bad situations beyond their control. Many have come too late to the table of life to even get the crumbs that are left."

"What can I do now? I guess it really is too late."

A slight light shone in Cora's eyes and her lips turned up a fraction at the corners. "Life is made up of many parts. No matter how small the effort, amends can be made. Major victories or minor instances of good are of equal measure in the eyes of the Lord."

Cora folded her wrinkled hands into her apron. "You haven't been a bad person, John. You've just been sleepwalking through most of your life. It's better to realize your shortcomings even now. If what I am told is true, you have made an effort with your family. You have touched them in a small way that may grow with time. Flowers sometimes flourish in the spring regardless of how much snow the winter has left behind."

John looked into Cora's eyes as she said, "Be in the present with me and let your feelings grow. It is not too late to create a future beyond this moment."

\*\*\*

Solitude had been John's ally for many years, but usually not in these picturesque surroundings. It was better to be here with natural and man-made beauty. He was used to being trapped by the sterile walls of the city.

In the late afternoon he took his grandfather's rowboat out onto the placid waters of the lake. Threading the bisected bloodworm on the hook was difficult, but the memory of having done this before with his father led to a serene pleasure. The hook broke the surface of the slightly chilled water on the way to the foot-high grasses where the fish liked

29

to hide. The small weight sinkers and the light nylon fishing line gave him just the right feel for the nibbles that jostled his hand when the fish decided to be daring. The sun played on the brim of his broad canvas hat as his tinted glasses adjusted to the light. It was calm and quiet as his index finger rested on the fishing line anticipating the gentle vibration. The float pulled beneath the surface, and he finally jerked the rod upward to hook his prey. Waiting for the fish to hit was like meditation with your eyes open he thought. All senses seem to flow to the fingers in a primal handshake with the worn, cork handle of the rod.

***

John thought there was nothing better than baked largemouth bass and perch pan-fried with a cornmeal crust. The smells still permeated Cora's kitchen an hour after John's triumphant return from the dock with the haul of six fish large enough to keep.

A vintage table with a chrome edged, yellow Formica top and six tubular chrome-base chairs with vinyl seats dominated the sunroom. Cora and John sat looking out at the ripples of the lake coming toward them from the south. In preparation for the meal, John had summoned up distant lessons of cleaning fish with his father. He used his grandfather's knives that were honed to a perfect edge for this purpose. Cora made skillet cornbread with whole kernels of corn and a dark tan crust on top, green beans with garlic and tomatoes, and freshly squeezed lemonade.

Cora rolled up the bamboo shades as the sun set. The slanted ribbons of clouds to the north reflected the deep orange glow of the sun receding behind the trees. The slight breeze stopped as the sun went down. The still lake silhouetted the dark green aluminum rowboat tethered to the dock. As the last vestiges of the day sank into the lake's edge, the colors morphed into deep blues, purples and lavenders that made the water appear to be efflorescent. John heard the loons on the lake trumpeting their good night song to the strains of a Brahms' Lullaby. He was almost happy. He had forgotten what this felt like.

As they went back into the living room, Cora asked John to try to crank up the four-foot tall Brunswick gramophone player that sat in the corner. It had been idle for over two years since Cora's husband had died. Samuel Cooper Sessions had bought the player years ago to soothe his infant son and help him sleep at night. He transferred the heavy gramophone to the lake house soon after moving in. It was a luxury in a modest home. Stored below the player were upright drawers full of vintage, quarter inch thick Edison one sided disks and newer Columbia Gramophone Company LPs. They contained family entertainment such as "That Wonderful Mother Of Mine", and the flipside "I Can't See The Good In Good-bye".

At the bottom of the files of original pressings were a few smaller recordings labeled "Make Your Own Record" and one hand-signed "Bill Schall 1938". The square brown sleeve with the six-inch hole in the middle held a scratchy greeting from the past from Uncle Bill. He had sung with The Harmony Four from 1937 to 1938 and was on the recording of "Just As Your Mother Was". The Brunswick player had an elegant arched silver arm with steel needles. He had never seen a player this old in such pristine shape. The disks spun on the spindle resulting in a sound that was an ethereal mix of marching bands, sweet hymns, Beethoven and Billy Holiday. John could hear the passage of time.

***

John retired to Jimmy's bedroom. The central piece of furniture in the guest room was the dark stained mahogany dresser with attached mirror surrounded by ornate scrollwork.

On the wall opposite the wrought iron bed there was a grouping of photos of uncles, aunts, and grandparents soon to be lost in time. At the center was a sepia tone photo of Samuel and Cora. Grandmother was in her Sunday best in a long, pleated skirt and a white, lacy, long sleeved blouse with a high collar up her slender, elegant neck. Grandfather was dapper in his dark pinstripe suit and the heavily starched white shirt and bow tie. They both had that look from old photographs of a smile trying to break through the formal pose, forever etched by the flash on the top of the huge wood box camera.

John's head hit the down pillow and he floated quickly into a deep sleep surrounded by the remnants of other lives more fulfilled than his. Even though he had achieved certain successes he had not let family have a place in his life. Now that he had started to let people through the protection of his walls, he had started to find peace. For the first time in weeks he had no dreams.

***

The next morning, the lacy curtains in the room did not hold back the direct sun. He rose with slightly aching bones that somehow felt refreshed despite his age and circumstance. He hurt less than yesterday. The smell of coffee and warm, white-iced cinnamon buns aroused his senses beyond his normal muted world.

Cora asked, "Did you sleep well?"

"Better than I can remember sleeping before. I think I will

be alright."

He was home and beginning to live again.

# My Dad Could Climb Couches

## By: John Stipa

I've always held stock in the saying "A man's home is his castle." It's a profound statement, especially if one considers that by using the word castle to express the analogy, the creator is suggesting that is also where a man is King.

It would be fun to take the analogy literally. But it'd be even more fun if taken figuratively or by using substitutes. A man's home is his cave, or his fort, igloo, domain, his safe harbor. Or just plain... his.

A man's home is his. Period. Stick a fork in it, done, take it out of the oven and serve it. No need to garnish it with a fancy table setting or improve it with spice or sauce. Just let everyone accept that it's what's for dinner, at his Arthurian round table if he so chooses. The dish eats just fine, like a King Henry VIII drumstick.

Speaking of Englishmen, I found that the saying dates to 1628 when Sir Edward Coke, lawyer and politician, wrote into English common law the legal precept that no one may enter a man's home unless by invitation:

"For a man's house is his castle, and
each man's home is his safest refuge."

It's a simple concept, succinct, to the point, and core to a
man's proximity on the planet, his reason for being, his North
Star. It gives clarity to his life, a sense of grounding… and
function; a purpose that may, if he's lucky, involve a family:
the purpose of being a producer, provider, protector, and
procreator.

My father was one such lucky man, whose only mistake
was forgetting he wasn't governed by English common law as
written by Sir Edward. No, my father lived in an Italian
household, which meant he was governed by Italian common
mother-in-law, as written by my grandmother.

My mother and grandmother jointly purchased the house
we grew up in in the early 1950's. Jointly as in my mom put
up the entire down payment and did all the housework.
Grandmom sat in a chair by the TV watching wrestling,
barking commands for my mom to change the channel, deliver
meals, or listen to rants on everything that was wrong with the
world. At the top of that list was my father.

It could go down in history as the worst decision by a
newly married man to move in with his Italian mother-in-law
instead of building his own castle. Granted, that may have

been the way it was done back in their day, but hindsight is 20/20, or so reads another truism. He could have looked around and realized everyone else in the neighborhood made the financial commitment to go it on their own. Why didn't he? I can't answer that. He could have built a moat to keep Grandmom out, or mounted vats of molten tar at all the turrets or positioned archers between the battlements.

Maybe it was lack of money, or maybe he simply liked the place - we'll never know. But what we do know is that he made a lot of improvements. And that's when my dad moved to the top of the rant list and became Grandmom Enemy #1.

You could argue that my dad just liked to tinker or that he was eccentric, take your pick, but what you cannot say is that he was lazy. He built a detached two-car garage at the back of the property with a separate room on the side where he stored construction equipment. On the roof, he added a pigeon coop (here's where the eccentric argument gains momentum). Why he did that, I cannot fathom. The only thing that makes sense is his family had pigeons in Italy and he was trying to recreate aspects of his parents' house in the old country. Didn't matter to Grandmom. She hated the idea of flying rats being provided a hotel on the property. And that he fed them was complete insanity.

I remember my sister and me hiding under the piano bench in the family room when my dad first pitched the idea to Grandmom and Mom. His occupancy contract with Grandmom must have contained some full disclosure clause that required he apply for a "Granmit" (short for Grandmom permit) and it had to receive two-thirds vote to make it through committee. Whatever the endorsement process, the pigeon coop did not go over well. I may need to fact check this, but this may have been where the term filibuster originated. I looked up the definition:

> "Act in an obstructive manner in legislature, especially by speaking at inordinate length."

I guess technically, that's what happened, but it doesn't come anywhere close to describing *the way* it happened. The definition just doesn't convey the ferocity of the battle. Grandmom was obstructive, that's for sure, but the definition makes it sound as if it is typically done in a mannered way. Well, I may have been a kid, but even I knew there was nothing mannerly about flinging her flabby arms in the air in defiance of the proposal, and her roaring like a wildebeest will never pass for speaking. The only thing that's accurate is that it went on for an inordinate length of time.

The longer my dad argued for the benefits, the louder

Grandmom belched mouthfuls of spaghetti at him. It was like a heavyweight boxing match, only medieval in intensity. Each combatant would take the other's best shot, then reload and fire back. A punch for a punch. An insult for an insult. If he stomped his foot, she did a belly flop. If she slammed her fist on the table, he jumped up onto the couch and bounced on it like a trampoline.

Can I just interject here that in an Italian household, the couches were covered by see-through plastic, to protect them from spills and such. To put your feet up on the couch was blasphemy. To *climb onto* on the couch had no equal description of wickedness. But to *jump* from one cushion to another, gaining altitude with each spring, with intentional animated agility, all the while taunting Grandmom with Italian curse words, bringing it to a crescendo by landing on the floor in a thunderous "thoom" of a two-footed landing that even the Incredible Hulk would envy, was so beyond sacrilegious defamation, that it must have been the only time in all of history that one man violated all 10 of the commandments simultaneously by one gesture. Every statue in Rome fell over that evening in belief that the apocalypse was near.

Grandmom ran from the room, arms flailing high above her head, into her bedroom and slammed the door shut. My poor mother just placed the palm of her hand to her forehead and shook her head slowly while saying the rosary to try and exorcise the demons that had taken over my father that evening.

Dad built the pigeon coop and they came. The pigeons came and they ate. And they shit. Everywhere and on everything. It was disgusting. But it was beautiful too. I don't know what biological purpose a pigeon serves in the grand scheme of nature. We never witnessed it, that's for sure. But when my dad came home from work in his pick-up truck every day at 5 o'clock, the pigeons took flight and met him at the bottom of the driveway and flew in formation above him, like The Blue Angels welcoming home their great commander and hero. The Arthurian knight who went to war with one of the deadliest dragons known to any young boy, the man who had fought for their existence had returned home safely from a day away from the castle. All shit aside, that was a pretty damn glorious thing to witness.

King Arthur could wield Excalibur. My dad could climb couches.

# Bless the Child

## By: John Stickney

I listen to the silence

which is my child

sleeping,

breath soft

as a pillow

that has never

been used.

If I could press

my ear

against

the pillow

all I would hear

is silence:

against that breath,

word

after

word

of wondrous

silence.

Blessed breath,
blessed silence.

# The Blue Chair

## By: Suzy Tenenbaum

The big worries were always there. Would my son Luke get a new heart in time? Would his lungs and kidneys hold out as his heart failed? Or would they deteriorate to the point that he would no longer be eligible for transplantation? If a new heart became available, would he survive the operation? Even then, how long would it extend his life? Yes, the big worries were always there.

But some days the little worries took over and the question of whether I would get a turn to sit in the blue chair topped that list.

The blue chair was a high-backed, deeply cushioned place of comfort in Luke's hospital room. It was strategically positioned under the only window in the room. From it, you could see Luke, the TV, and out into the hall. A footrest popped out when you pulled the bar on the side allowing you to sink into the softness to take a good nap. And, unfortunately, it became my ex-husband Jay's favorite chair.

Most days, Jay and I walked the two miles to Childrens'

Hospital from our side-by-side apartments in Shadyside, PA. As we entered Luke's room, I would go to the bed, give Luke a hug, and ask how his night went. Jay headed straight for the blue chair.

There was also a wooden chair with a beige plastic seat in the room. Every day in the afternoon I would pull the beige chair up to Luke's bedside and we would play games; either Rummicube or Mancala. I didn't mind that chair at all during those times, but the seat back was not very high, so napping was impossible.

It was not often that I got a turn to sit in the blue chair. Only on the rare days when Jay was golfing, or went out on an errand, or the blessed, but few days, when he flew back to Vermont, was I able to savor it's comfy caress. Ah, the natural light! A small stream of sunshine would light the pages of my book, and the wide, padded arms were just right for holding the hand-written instructions for how to do a cable for the purple vest I was knitting for my five-year-old daughter who was back home.

A few times, when Jay left Luke's room, often for a smoke, I moved into the blue chair. But I was scared. I knew Jay didn't like the beige chair and I knew he'd be annoyed seeing me in "his" chair. When I did get a chance to sit in the chair, I spent some of my precious time worrying about being in it, and the look that Jay would give me. As soon as I got out of the chair to get ice for Luke, or go to use the bathroom, Jay would be back in that spot when I returned. This went on for four months.

We even had struggles about when to leave the hospital in the evening. It usually wasn't a problem when spring arrived, when it stayed light later. But in the winter, when darkness set in around 4:30 pm, it was a big issue, at least for me. I didn't want to walk alone in Pittsburgh in the dark, feeling safer when Jay and I walked together. If I were tired at 8 pm or so, I'd ask him when he thought he might be ready to leave. Most days he said, "I don't know. I'm not sure." or "Maybe in a while." I don't recall him ever asking me, "When would you like to leave?" I don't think he cared. Rather, he cared to have things his way and leave when he wanted, after spending most of the day in that blue chair.

So many of my marital issues of years ago —power, passive aggression, and lack of fairness—were exemplified by that blue chair. I was aware of it as it happened, but just as in our marriage, I could not figure a way out.

The big worries in life are difficult enough, but sometimes it's the small things that get to you.

# Toby

## By: Lorraine Gilmore

"It feels as if this day started earlier than usual. Well, in some ways it did because I awoke several hours before it was time to get up. I hate when that happens. My mind churns with so many thoughts."

Speaking to no one but herself, Marge finished buttoning her blouse and pulled on her sweater. She walked into the kitchen and turned on the burner under the teakettle. As she was taking teabags from the cabinet, she felt soft fur against her leg.

"Good morning, Toby. You probably want some food in your dish."

*It's so easy to get the attention of my woman-friend. It's nice that she always seems to know what I want.*

Marge opened a can of tuna and flaked it into the dish beside the refrigerator.

"There you are. Enjoy"

*Yummy! Bumblebee Tuna instead of that Fancy Feast stuff. This must be a special day.*

Marge made a cup of tea and went to sit in the recliner. There was no hurry to fix her breakfast. She let out a loud sign and began to sip her tea.

"Living alone is not as much fun as I used to think it would be all those years ago. It's been a year since George died and I still miss him so much."

*M-e-e-ow-ow.*

The greeting was especially mournful this morning.

"Toby. I'll bet you'd like to sit on a nice, warm lap."

She reached over and picked up the tabby. As he felt her legs beneath him, he began to circle and press his paws against her. After doing this a few times, he curled up and put his head down.

*Gone are the days when I could jump up on a lap or a counter. Getting old is no fun at all. I wish I didn't have so many aches and pains.*

"This is nice. I miss having a warm body curled up against me. You heard me complain a lot about George. He was such a pain in the ass, but he was my pain in the ass and I miss him. In fifty-six years he never put his socks in the dirty clothes basket. They were always left on the floor for me to pick up."

*I miss my man-friend. He was never too busy for a cuddle and we always took naps.*

"You know, Toby, that man never washed a dish and couldn't find the laundry detergent in broad daylight. And, you couldn't pay him to go to Macy's or any other store. I used to envy wives who had a companion when they went shopping."

A tear rolled down Marge's cheek. As she stroked Toby's back, she avoided the growing bulge of the tumor on his spine. It was inoperable.

"I'm going to miss you too, Toby. You've been such a comfort to me this past year. The vet told me that it is not fair to have you linger now that the pain medication cannot give you any relief. "

Marge picked up Toby and put him in the kennel by the door.

*Well, I used to dread these trips because there was always a shot at the other end. Not anymore. Now the old man hooks me up to a tube and the liquid makes me all warm and cozy. All the pain goes away.*

The vet had told Marge to bring Toby in before office hours that morning and so the waiting room was empty. He heard the door open and came in right away.

"Good Morning, Marge. How is Toby today?"

"Not so good, Doc. I can tell that he is in a lot more pain than usual."

"Do you want to leave him with me or do you want to stay?"

"I don't want to leave him."

"Bring him into the exam room and you can hold him while I administer the anesthetic."

It was not as bad as Marge expected. Toby lay quietly in her arms as the anesthetic dripped into him. He appeared to go to sleep. After about fifteen minutes she could feel that he had stopped breathing. The vet used the stethoscope and could not hear any heartbeat. Marge was quietly crying with tears running down her cheeks.

The vet handed her a tissue.

"He's gone, Marge. How are you doing?"

"I'm glad that I was with him, but it was harder than I expected."

"Do you want to leave him with me?"

"No. I have a nice spot in the garden for his final resting place."

"Marge, we have a new litter of kittens at home. They'll be ready for new homes next week."

"I'd like that Doc. The house won't feel so empty and they'll keep me busy. I'll plan to come by the end of next week. Send me some pictures on my phone. I'll let you know which ones I want and plan to pick them up at the office."

"Works for me. You take care and I'll see you then.

Marge did as she said and while she did not forget Toby, the two new kittens brought a lot of fun to her empty house.

# Oak Trees and Acorns

## By: Claudia Blanchard

My dad loved adventure. The good, sporting kind of thrill. He won track and field events in high school, began downhill skiing in his forties and played tennis throughout his life. But when he aged into his eighties, and his world became smaller, he substituted getting into trouble for his adventurous past.

At the deli counter of the Publix supermarket in Bradenton, Florida, after the second or third jostling, my father boomed "stop bumping into me you fat cow."

Then came the woman's reply as she jabbed her finger into my dad's corpulent belly, "Who are you calling a fat cow?"

Joining in the fray came the jostling lady's husband's response, "Buddy, let's take this outside to the parking lot." Oh boy, I thought, a rumble, senior citizen style.

Trouble clung to my dad like insects on a car windshield. Late one morning, my stepmom answered the phone to a police officer's query, "This Mrs. Cines? We found your husband's car abandoned in the road, on Papermill Drive". Off on a morning bagel-run, my dad's car ran out of gas. Thumb out, he caught a ride to the nearest filling station. Having forgotten his cell phone again, he was at the mercy of everyone's good graces – the truck driver who picked him up, the police officer who found his car and hopefully, upon his return home, his wife.

Food was often at the center of my dad's misadventures. Now, my husband claims I've begun to channel him. To become the daughter of my father. Take, for instance, my time at the Publix supermarket deli counter in Estero, Florida, where I spotted nestled among the detritus of poppy seeds and bread crumbs, one lone, last plain bagel. Sensing another pair of eyes on this circle of goodness, I rushed in and grabbed it. The elderly gentleman behind me sighed. The New Yorker in me did a little victory dance. My husband was horrified. I replied with a smile and a shrug and a plain bagel in hand.

Oak trees and acorns.

# Color Me

## By: Terry L. Dismore

Color me with Love

Color me all the colors of the Rainbow to show my Success

Color me with a bright Future

Color me Without Labels and allow me to Blossom and Grow

Color me with Dreams; don't add any Limits or Seams

Color me with Hope and Optimism

Color me with Courage, Peace, and Grace

Color me with Vision, Revelation, and Innovation

Color me Caring, Daring, and Truthful

Color me surrounded with all the colors in the crayon box

Color me Human and Compassionate, please

Color me smothered in Hugs, Kisses, and Love

Color me Free, allowing me to be Adventurous

Allow me to Color me!

Color Me was originally published in P.A.R.E.N.T.S, Terry's first novel.

# A New House, A New Family

## By: Barbara Dullaghan

The office felt as gloomy as the cemetery outside. Besides the light from the door, there was only one small window about four feet up on the wall. Someone had hung a spider plant, which desperately needed more light and, I assumed, more water. Clenching the bouquet of yellow roses and baby's breath in my left hand, I leaned in towards the receptionist and asked again, "Is there any way you can please help me? I've come so far."

"I'm sorry, but I can't help you unless you know the lot number," she answered. "As you may know, this cemetery is huge and our database is on these index cards, but they're not organized by name."

I looked at the boxes and boxes of index cards and sighed deeply. Leaving the office, I thought I might walk around a bit and look at the gravestones. I only had about forty-five minutes before I had to return to the hotel to start my way back to Minneapolis. I had come a long way to my hometown to place a fresh bouquet of yellow roses on Ann's grave. The ground was soft from the recent rain and the trees heavy with new growth and dampness. I always loved this place. It was never scary to me, but always mysterious. Dark and quiet, kind of like Ann.

Ann was my mother's friend. They met as roommates in the hospital when both were receiving treatments for illnesses: my mother for a recurring lung issue, Ann for cancer. I remember very clearly the day my parents told me we were moving from our two-bedroom apartment to a house five miles away in North Tarrytown. Even at my young age, I knew a house was something they always wanted, but could never afford. I looked at Dad's gentle face as he started to talk about growing tomatoes in the backyard and roses in the front. Then, it was Mom's turn to talk about my walking to school and not taking the bus, making more friends and our family of three having room to spread out.

"Oh, and you will love the little room off your bedroom that looks out onto the river," Mom gushed. "It's just beautiful."

It was exciting for all of ten minutes. The next one was shocking to me.

"Ann is dying of cancer and needs someone to take care of her and her home," my mother continued. "Her mother just died before she went into the hospital and her male cousin will be moving out. We will be moving in with Ann. She needs our help."

"What?" I erupted, as my parents seemed to back away from me. "Ann? Didn't you just meet her? The woman I just met two weeks ago? Mom's roommate in the hospital? You take care of me! I take care of you! I don't want that to change!" I stormed off to my room.

Probably because of that outburst, preparing for the move was agonizing at times for our family. I was not the only one filled with trepidation. I overheard my parents discussing how things would change for our family; lack of privacy for them was a big concern. My father insisted on paying rent although my mother, a nurse, would be taking care of Ann. My parents tried to talk with me but I had made up my mind that the move was going to happen and I didn't want to discuss it.

We moved in two months later and it was a true eye-opener for me. A pretty white Cape Cod on the outside, the house had only one bathroom upstairs near the bedrooms. Heavy, dark drapes blocked the sunlight and the furniture was arranged with everything against the walls. I assumed that was so Ann would be able to walk easily through the house. Pictures of German ancestors lined the walls and the china dishes in the hutch were probably already antiques back then. This was clearly Ann's home. I wondered how we would make it our home too.

My parents moved into the master bedroom and Ann into her cousin's room so I could have hers. I loved my room. It looked out into the back yard with a lovely, full maple tree and the garden that would eventually include my father's beefsteak tomatoes and green beans. Attached to my room was a large walk-in closet with a window that looked out onto the Hudson River, about a mile down the hill. I still feel chills when I see that river. As a teenager gripped with anxiety, I always daydreamed about it taking me away. I could see the boats and the new bridge that was being built to connect Tarrytown to Nyack. It was a beautiful view and my favorite part of our house.

My parents were soon able to make the house their own by removing the heavy drapes and portraits, and painting the interior a much brighter light blue to replace the gloomy gray. They also added a coffee table and ottoman in the living room and Ann learned to maneuver around them.

It was fascinating to talk with Ann because she was totally blind. As a thirteen year old, I couldn't stop looking at her eyes, cloudy and completely useless. I always felt like she knew I was staring. I was always uncomfortable.

Ann was much older than my parents and yet she traveled into New York City twice a week on the train to work at the School for the Blind, accompanied by just her cane. She read profusely with her Braille machine and, I had to admit, she was very smart. She did try to teach me a little Braille and I remember doing a class project on that experience. We were alike in that we were both only children, a club one understands only if you are one. Both of us were fiercely independent and good problem solvers.

Which also meant that we did not always get along. I usually did my best to avoid her. Even after a year, I was still uncomfortable around her. She was so observant that I was sure she could see me and could even hear me breathing! I certainly did not appreciate it when I heard her tell my mom that she shouldn't let me talk back to her and that I should be grateful for all they had done for me. I turned around, went to my room, and slammed the door. Clearly, Ann had never lived with an angst-ridden teenager before. I felt it was very unfair of her to judge me. I remember once moving the ottoman out away from the chair so she banged into it as she passed me. I have never forgotten I did that and still cringe when I think of it.

When Ann died a year later, she kindly left the house to my parents. It must have been hard for her to share her home with us. It also must have been difficult for her to rely so heavily on someone else. And it must have been very challenging to deal with me, a highly verbal and dramatic teenage girl. As I reflect, I feel like we had somewhat of a sibling relationship when we entered each other's lives to form this new family. I had been the center of my family's attention, as had she. And then, suddenly, neither of us were.

I learned many lessons from this woman of substance and I felt crushed that I hadn't been able to leave the flowers on her grave. But, just recently, I told a good friend about the story and she suggested I look online with the information that I had. I knew Ann's name, her mother's maiden name, and the cemetery. We finally found the lot number for the gravesite. I was so excited to have the information but when I returned to the cemetery with a fresh bouquet of beautiful purple astromelias, I walked all around the section and could not find the grave. I placed the flowers in the middle of the section, saying, "Well, this is for all of you." I returned to my car, feeling defeated again, and drove on the dirt road to leave. I glanced one more time to my left and, there was Ann's gravestone! Jumping out of the car, I ran to retrieve the flowers and finally placed them by her grave. All I could think of saying was, "Sorry for moving the ottoman."

I think Ann would appreciate the flowers and the thought. After all, we were family.

# Lemons and Pickles

## By: Lee Norman Mehler

"If life gives you lemons, make lemonade."

Aunt Sadie had a tendency to repeat the antiquated sayings that she had heard for many years and used them often.

She thought this as Uncle Sol lumbered through the creaking screen door from the Sunshine Pickle Factory earlier than expected. He stripped down to his tee shirt and shorts, grabbed the usual beer and tumbled into the couch with the indentation where he had sat for the last thirty-five years. He was silent as normal, but somehow Sadie thought his quietness had a different look. Sol's lined face was an open book. Sadie could easily read every crease. His usual scowl was replaced by something softer. There was a distant look in his eyes. It was too early for his sacred New York Mets game so he sat staring at the blank 12" Motorola TV screen slowly sipping the Schlitz chilling his arthritic hand.

"What's the matter, Sol?"

"Nuttin'," he grunted.

"I know you. Usually you pout when you come home. But

you seem poutier today."

Sol sighed loudly, not wanting to answer to anyone.

"Tell your little Sadie what's the matter Solly Wolly."

"You know I can't resist when you sweet talk me, Sadie." It seemed longer but it only took a few seconds for Sol to start spilling his guts. "They want to promote me at the factory and I'm just not sure."

"What's wrong with a few extra dollars each month, honey?"

"This is unchartered territory for me. I'm comfortable after years in the Gherkin department and they want to bump me up to the Kosher Dills. I don't know if I can take the pressure."

"How do you mean, dear?"

"Gherkins are easy for me! I'm used to the slightly sweet vinegar processing of those small delicacies. The larger Half Sour Kosher Dills terrify me! It's just too much responsibility!"

"Maybe you should sleep on it. Don't make a rash decision without letting it marinate overnight. It's the love you put into each pickle spear that counts. As Grandma Betsy used to say 'size doesn't matter.'"

Grandma Betsy was the matriarch of the family. She had taken her position on the production line in the Gherkin

Department right after the factory had its ribbon cutting in Suffolk, Long Island in 1923. Sol had spent many holidays tagging along admiring Grandmother's eye for the perfect pickle. Sol had inherited his slowly nurtured skill for spotting the best green Gherkin with its gentle curve and slightly rough texture.

"Why are you so nervous about the change, dear? At some philosophical level, a pickle is just a pickle. Large, small, dark green, light green. It all leaves a sour taste in my mouth."

Sol's neck veins throbbed and bulged. "You don't understand the subtleties of this profession, Sadie. You don't understand what this means to the family. There is a pride in our history with this product, this company, this town built on these sour gems.

"But why are you scared, Sol?"

"The conveyor belt moves faster! Those suckers are bigger! My eyes have been trained for the smaller scale Gherkins. I'm afraid I'll miss an imperfection. When I do my shift on the tasting line I don't know that I can distinguish a sour from a half sour, or a Kosher from a non-Kosher."

Sadie's eyes welled up as she held back the tears. She couldn't decide if she was on the verge of crying because of her husband's raw emotions or to stop laughing at the absurdity of this conversation.

"Take a deep breath, my love. Close your eyes and imagine what life would be like if you were in the business of making pork sausage. It could be a whole lot worse, Sol.

"The game starts in ten minutes. Sit there and relax. I will go inside to make your favorite dinner. Meatloaf and mashed potatoes, fresh squeezed lemonade and apple pie with vanilla ice cream for dessert. No pickles tonight!"

Sol took a deep breath and exhaled slowly. How did this woman know how to say just the right thing at just the right time? Might as well turn on the tube and watch his Mets lose another one. If there was a miracle, his world might be a little less sour tomorrow.

# Paper

## By: John Stickney

If I could eat paper, I tell my wife,

I would not go hungry.

My wife cooks "Newspaper Surprise."

My children watch TV, refusing their portions.

I ache, my stomach swells with the disasters

Of last night's news.

I burp an auto accident.

I hiccup a terrorist attack.

My heart's aflame.

Arson is suspected.

# Sandwich Generation

## By: Suzy Tenenbaum

"You're putting your mascara on wrong," she says to me. "Come into my room and I'll show you the brush I use. You have to get into the corners."

Like a compliant child, I follow my 94-year-old mother into her room where she opens the closet and pulls out her gold trimmed china tray where her makeup is carefully displayed. She pulls out a tiny brush that she holds up for me. "See how the brush bristles are thick?

"I see that—thanks Mom. I think I have a mascara brush like that, so I'll try to use it," I respond without much conviction. Then I turn and leave.

Sixty-four years old and I'm still getting make up lessons. I am both annoyed and also touched. How many of my friends are lucky enough to get makeup advice from their moms? Since Helen is still beautiful, I want to listen to her beauty secrets.

But her comments still sting a bit. They're made more annoying by the fact that when my daughter, Sasha, visited last April, she commented, "Mom, I don't think your mascara is right. Maybe you want to try Clump Crusher mascara. It comes in a green tube."

Clearly I am the sandwich generation between two beauties. Several folks have told me Sasha has my mom's glamour, so I guess I'll listen to both these women who seem to have inside information on attaining beauty. But one thing I know for sure: I had more confidence when I thought I already knew how to put on mascara, and doesn't confidence add a special shine?

Being in the sandwich generation keeps me on my toes, because roles can vacillate within minutes. Whenever we are dressing to go out, my mom calls, "Suzy, can you come into my room for a minute? Please help me decide what I should wear." Then she steps back and listens while I suggest outfits, and then she waits until I choose one.

"You haven't worn that for a while," I say, "and you have the matching jacket if you get chilly." If I reassure Mom that she will be warm enough, she agrees, except for yesterday when she said she was too hot. Sometimes my mother is my child. Sometimes she is my recalcitrant child. If I seem too invested in an outfit suggestion, she says, "Don't be so bossy!" and then I know she is back in the mother role keeping me in my place.

Last week, my mother told me I might like to consider getting lipstick with a bit more orange in it. I'm considering her advice. Likewise, she is considering my advice regarding her brother Allen who has been calling her almost daily. Recently I overheard Alan tell her to stop reading the New York Times "because it's fake news. You think you're smarter than the rest of us, don't you," he said to her. Helen became upset and I heard her respond in a shrill voice. I walked in at that moment and loudly said that I needed her in the kitchen and she got off the phone. She was grateful for the support. She asked me, "What do I tell him the next time he calls?" We then made a script and she wrote some notes to help her remember for the next phone call. Advice goes both ways: She tells me about mascara. I suggest ways to resist a bully brother.

Next month Sasha visits, and I'm eager to hear her beauty secrets! On our last phone call she asked which moisturizer I was using at night. I can imagine after she leaves I will have a new product to help me "reduce the appearance of fine lines."

There are advantages to being in the sandwich generation.

# Breakfast with a King

## By: Diane Pascoe

I had just hunted down the last piece of eggshell playing hide-and-seek in the gooey yellow mixture, which was now ready to be scrambled. The sausages were sizzling, and the bagels had defrosted for toasting. I was all set for our post-prom breakfast guests.

It was 7:30 am, and the graduates were still sleeping off their *Café Luna* dinners and nursing their electric-slide-sore tootsies. Sometime during the wee hours, high heels had been abandoned by the young women in favor of flip-flops, as evidenced by the collection of footwear at the front door.

The prom was all about the boy matching his girlfriend's dress color—one shade off and the date was doomed before it started. Our son Braden's friend, Adam, wore a tux, now rolled into a ball on the floor, which was wrapped with his Caribbean turquoise bow tie and vest, a perfect match for the Caribbean turquoise dress worn by his date, Pamela. Braden's Ferrari red vest and tie were identical to the color of Missy's nail polish and dress. For the record, Missy's real name was

Suzanne, but long ago I had decided to call all my son's girlfriends "Missy" when speaking to them, so that I didn't accidentally use the name of a previous girlfriend. The lineup of girlfriends switched out periodically, so I was always worried that I would be one step behind in his dating life. An all-purpose name like Missy, though admittedly a bit impersonal, proved to be much safer.

Just as I started slicing the bagels, I heard teenage footsteps come bounding down the stairs, breaking the calm of the early morning —thud, thud, thud.

"Good morning, Mom," said a bright and chipper Braden as he surveyed the kitchen. "We need to have people over for breakfast more often. You haven't made me a hot breakfast since I was three."

*Heavens to pancakes!* Maybe he was 3, maybe he was 13— I had no idea when I had last served a hot meal. But this was not the time to debate the history of Pascoe hot breakfasts because getting the food on the table required the precision timing of a rocket launch at Cape Canaveral. Braden would need to consider this hot meal a special event, like the appearance of a comet, because there were fourteen boxes of cereal in the pantry, including *All Bran Buds* for regularity, that needed to be eaten first.

73

The sleepy-eyed graduates slowly wandered into the kitchen, taking their places at the table. I served them my first breakfast dish—a special "Fruit Fiesta" concoction, which had been marinating overnight. I was quite impressed with myself because I was really in the swing of post-prom breakfast production—I had even put the bagels under the oven broiler instead of toasting them in shifts in the toaster, just to be more efficient.

"So how was the prom?" I asked to get the breakfast conversation started.

"Ya know what?" said Adam. "Andy was crowned prom king."

A prom king at our very own breakfast table!

"Andy, did you get a crown?" I asked.

From under the table, Andy brought out his prize—a blue-fuzzy-fabric creation with silver trim which he plopped on his head. It was too big for him, obviously meant for a king with a bigger head than Andy, but surely not a bigger heart.

"How did you get selected as prom king, Andy? Did you have to sing or dance or act out a scene from Hamlet?"

Before Andy could answer, Braden jumped into the conversation. "Nah, he didn't have to do anything. He just got the most votes. Everyone really likes Andy."

74

Our king was not only popular, but very modest.

"So, who was the prom queen?" I continued, confident that at least one of our lovely female guests had been chosen.

"There were three—a queen and two princesses," said Braden, naming young women I didn't know. Voters had apparently overlooked Pamela and Suzanne. I had personally heard Suzanne growl like Simba in *The Lion King,* a role she played in elementary school, and nobody could have performed better than her had there been a talent competition.

All this talk of prom queens reminded me of my own twelfth-grade event in which I had been the second-runner up prom princess. Being the spare-to-the-heir impressed my three disbelieving sisters at the time, but Braden, on learning of this feat, pointed out that because it was a convent school, it was a dubious achievement. He did have a point.

I was so busy thinking about my own long-ago prom that I failed to notice a smoky haze emanating from the oven, smelling remarkably like burnt bagels. As the smoke hit the ceiling, it set off the smoke alarm, ensuring that our guests were now fully awake. *Ohmygod—the bagels!* I opened the oven door to see five cremated bagels lying dead on the baking sheet. I quickly tossed their blackened remains into the water-filled sink to silence the screeching smoke alarm, then I sliced more bagels and slipped this second batch under the broiler.

Unbelievably, I flunked toasting a second time. This second batch had toasted faster than I anticipated, and I was left with *another* batch of burnt bagels, proving once again, that my timing was completely off.

I refused to believe that toasting bagels required higher level cooking skills, so I tried one last time, watching the bagels closely as they toasted this time, then rescuing them at exactly the right moment. Luckily, all the other breakfast dishes came off without a hitch. Mission accomplished!

A senior prom comes along once in a boy's life, and a king comes to breakfast very rarely. All in all, the meal turned out very well. Martha Stewart may never have burned her bagels twice, but I doubt she's been lucky enough to serve prom royalty.

# Gracie's Web

## By: John Stipa

Stan Palmer elbowed his lanky frame through the crowded, smoke filled room. Reaching the bar, he pulled out a stool and wedged his way onto the empty seat. "Evening Fitzy, T.G.I.F."

"Hey! Stan the Man," Dan Fitzgerald called out, flipping a white bartender's towel over his beefy shoulder. Without asking, the former defensive tackle grabbed a mug and slapped the tap of the draft beer. When the white foam climbed to the rim, he popped the lever to the "off" position and slid the mug so that it stopped in front of his favorite Friday night customer. "How you been? You're late, it's almost seven."

"Got hung up at work," Stan said, opening a pack of smokes. "Tough case to prosecute. Teenage girl being abused by her stepfather. Her word against his. Makes you wanna puke." He slugged down the beer in one chug and set the mug down harder than necessary. "Not sure I'm up to it."

Fitzy poured Stan another, but an empty mug came back

before he could walk away. Fitzy's bushy red eyebrows arched. "Hmm. Gonna be one of *those* kind of nights, is it? Flush it for now, man. If he's dirty, you'll nail him." He leaned on the bar. "You always do. Remember Ernie McMillan? Even I didn't think you'd be able to prove him guilty."

"What a punk," Stan said, remembering the case of rape. "Town Councilman's son and our classmate. Even in first grade everybody knew he was trouble. Thought he was tough shit. Never could keep his mouth shut. All I had to do was stoke him a bit on the stand. His ego did the rest."

"Bet he squeals loud in prison," Fitzy smiled. "Pretty boy like that."

Stan laughed and high-fived his giant friend. "Thanks man, I needed that." He tossed the cigarettes to Fitzy. "Here, chuck these. Don't let me start—ever. You know...speaking of squealing, you just gave me an idea on how to catch Chester the Molester. Check it out. We lure him into the bar and get him drunk until he passes out. Then while he sleeps, we surgically implant electrodes into the slimy bastard's testicles."

"Yeah, we can be like secret agents on a mission," Fitzy said, pretending to hide behind the beer taps. "We'll need code names."

"I'll be Night Train," Stan said. "You can be Agent Orange."

"I'll administer the shots of whiskey," Fitzy said. "You can do the implanting."

Stan paused, furrowing his brow. "Thanks, dude. Appreciate the generosity."

"Don't mention it," Fitzy said, an ear-to-ear smile on his face.

"We give the detonator to the girl," Stan said. "If Chester tries anything, she hits a button. We stake out the emergency room and lock up the first guy who staggers in with fried balls. Case closed."

Fitzy's belly laugh could be heard across the room. "That's funny, but something tells me you got a real plan."

"Working on it, but I'll promise you this, Chester's goin' down, dude."

"I think I hear the cell door clangin' shut already," Fitzy said, and plopped a bowl of peanuts in front of Stan. "Had dinner yet?"

"Nope," Stan replied, his fingernail's scraping the bottom of the bowl. With his other hand, he shoved the mug closer to Fitzy. "She here yet?"

"Yeah, already chewed up and spit out three shmunzers," Fitzy said, refilling the empty glass. "She's a piranha, dude. Personally, I don't see what you see in her other than she has legs up to her neck."

"What else does she need?" Stan said, holding out a cupped hand.

Like a shuffleboard puck, Fitzy slung the mug across the bar, slapping it into Stan's palm. "How 'bout somebody yanking her claws and grinding down those fangs? You only come in once a week, but I see her all the time. She's a black widow spider. That blue dress is her trap and when you get sucked in, she strikes. I had a special fire extinguisher installed behind the bar just to put out the flames on the guys she shoots down."

"Yeah, but she's an awesome dancer," Stan said, draining a third mug. He wiped his mouth on his sleeve. "I love blue."

"Like that's a requirement for a long lasting relationship." Fitzy rubbed a scalp full of Brillo-pad red hair. "You know, for a smart lawyer-type, you sure are freakin' stupid."

"Hopeless romantic."

"Okay Busby, you keep waiting for her to ask you to dance."

"You mean Gatsby."

"You knew what I meant," Fitzy said and refilled Stan's mug. "Here, this one's on the Fitz. And then you're cut off."

"Grouch," Stan muttered, sticking his face in the foam and turning to survey the dance floor.

In the corner of the dance floor, a blond woman tested the stretch of her short blue dress in several directions at once. Young and full of energy, she wasn't afraid to let it rip. Her dance partner was a short guy with glasses and comb-over hair that had come unglued. He moved with his tongue in his cheek trying to stay in step with the music. Compared to the woman, he looked like he would soon blow a gasket. At one point, he attempted a 360-degree spin, only to find she was gone. For an awkward moment, he stood there searching the crowd and patting down his hair before scurrying away like a cockroach under the stove.

Stan's eyes followed the woman walking along the back wall. Her confident stride parted the crowd. To his alarm, she turned and approached him at the bar. She mounted the stool next to Stan, lit up a cigarette and faced the dance floor, scoping unsuspecting prey.

A man in an open-collared shirt, gold chains and fuzzy chest slid in between Stan and the woman.

"Hey beautiful," Fuzzy said, his voice velvety smooth.

"Saw you dancing with that bozo. Care to dance with someone who knows what he's doing out there?"

The woman didn't address the man, but spoke over his shoulder to Stan instead. "Hey there, tall, dark and somewhat unrepugnant. You come here every Friday. What do you think? Should I dance with the Missing Link?"

Stan eyed the man in tight pants. "The stock price for testosterone must be on the rise." He stuck his nose into the foam of his mug and took a big swig.

Fuzzy turned, inhaled on his cigarette, and blew a stream of foul smoke at Stan. "Anyone ever tell you that you look like Jimmy Stewart?"

Stan lowered the mug from his mouth, beer dribbling down his chin. His eyes bulged as he realized he was going to sneeze with the mouthful. Choking and snorting, he spewed beer all over the bar. Fuzzy backed away, trying not to get sprayed. Blondie started laughing.

"Come on," Blondie said. She grabbed Fuzzy's hand and led him to the dance floor.

"Smooth, Stan, real smooth," Fitzy said, tossing a towel on the spill. "Normally, I have to hose guys down after an encounter with Spider Lady. You can do it all by yourself."

"Go jump in the lake, you big lummox." Tossing some

bills on the bar, Stan lurched for the exit.

***

In the dingy hallway of his apartment complex, Stan leaned against the door to his place, trying to figure out why the key would not go into the lock. He knocked, but no one answered. As he fumbled around, a quiet, but deep voice snuck up on him.

"Hey good lookin,' welcome home."

Over his shoulder, Stan spotted a scraggly looking woman in zipper-happy cargo pants, high top Chuck Taylor sneakers and a droopy grey sweatshirt from Yale. She spied over the top of stylish glasses, doing her best to part bangs of jet-black hair that refused to stay out of her face.

"Oh, hello," he mumbled. He resumed wrestling with the lock and key, then stopped. Scrunching up his face, he added: "Tanya." Many years earlier, Stan had helped Tanya obtain a restraining order against her ex-husband when no one else would take the case. Not that it did any good. When the creep came cruising for trouble, she hid in Stan's apartment. Twenty-three at the time, she was a few years younger than Stan and worked in the diner. She couldn't afford the court costs. It was no big deal to Stan; he never bothered to send a bill.

Stooping over, he squeezed his eyes shut then opened them, trying to focus on the task. "How's my neighbor these days?"

"I'm good…now that you're here."

Stan stood up and turned around, his upper body moving in slow motion as if it were one piece, the key frozen in one hand, his eyes wide and wary.

"My computer is acting up again," she continued. "Can you come over?"

"It's just another virus. Run that program I showed you last time."

"I don't trust myself. Can't you fix me up?"

He returned to the battle, to no avail. Placing his palms on the wall, he banged his head on the door. "Gracie, where are you when I need you?"

"She's at my place, Stan," Tanya chirped. "You were late and she got hungry so I cooked her dinner. She's doing her homework."

Stan faced her. Peering through the stringy bangs were a set of seductive blue eyes Cleopatra would have killed for. He heard a subtle intake of breath and realized it was his own. Recovering, he opened his arms and offered a hug. "Tanya, thank you. What would I do without you?"

"Oh, probably starve, go homeless or fall victim to some unscrupulous man-killer."

Expecting some grungy smell, he was surprised when a lovely aroma of Freesia filled his lungs as they embraced. They had been cross-the-hall neighbors for years, but he couldn't remember ever being this close to her. "Ever since Rebecca left," he said, "you've been a wonderful friend. Gracie thinks you're the best."

Her arms tightened around his back as she pressed her body into his. He held her closer, enjoying the comfort of her warmth. A muffled sob drifted by his ear sending tension up his spine. When they parted, her fluttering eyes darted to the floor, but not before he detected a bit of moisture. "Hey, you all right? Something in your eye?"

She turned away quickly and plunged her key in the lock of her door. "No, I'm fine. It's…allergies." She turned the knob and opened the door. "I'll tell Gracie you're home. Goodnight, Stan." The door closed with a click.

He stood alone in the hallway, tie undone, shirt untucked, key still in hand, feeling very confused. He mouthed in a meek voice: "Goodnight, Tanya."

\*\*\*

"Hello, Capezio Dance? Hey, my name is Stan. I'm

looking to take lessons. I'm thirty-eight and a beginner-" A pause as the other party interrupted. "Oh, I see, well, thank you anyway." Stan clicked the phone off and crossed another studio's name off the list.

"What am I going to do, Gracie?" He said to his fourteen-year-old daughter. "It doesn't seem to want to work out for me. Every place I've called is either too far away or booked up."

Lying on her stomach, half her attention on her math homework, the other half on *Gilmore Girls*, Gracie was a fair-skinned teen in patched jeans and rainbow socks. Except for the pigtails and braces, she resembled Stan. She closed the text book and looked up with big brown eyes.

"Why all of a sudden this urge to learn to dance, Dad? Got a hot date?"

"There's this woman at Fitzy's and the only way to get to know her is to hang with her on the dance floor."

"What about connecting with her intellectually or having something in common?"

"Dancing is what we'll have in common."

Gracie wrinkled up her freckly face. "Why don'tcha go to Miss Ginny?"

"I thought she closed up shop right after you stopped

taking lessons."

"Nuh-uh. The girl I baby-sit for, Siobahn, she goes there."

"Is she listed in the Yellow Pages?"

"Nuh-uh. Word of mouth."

"Did she move her studio?"

"Nuh-uh. Still uses her basement."

"But she teaches kids."

"Uh-huh."

"Gracie, you, as will your future boyfriends, thank me, if I refuse to allow you to speak like a Troglodyte. So will you please stop grunting?"

"Sorry…Father."

"Thank you. Now, about Miss Ginny. Does she have anything that I—"

"Father," Gracie interrupted, "do you recall what you yourself pontificated when I first embarked with Miss Ginny? No? Then indulge me dear parental one. In your own immortal words, however superfluous they may have been, at four or forty-four, dance is, in the final analysis, simply locomotion of the body, with or without music. And, if you're little grey cells are cramping over my meaning, let me translate for you: dance is just dance. Father."

As Stan gaped, Gracie turned back to the on-screen

bickering of Rory and Loreli, smacking her feet together as she twisted the ends of her pigtails.

***

The next Friday, Stan burst into the apartment and hurled his briefcase into the corner. His coat went over the back of a kitchen chair, knocking it over. His mangled tie hit the floor.

"Dad," Gracie said, "what's wrong?"

"Wrong? Everything's wrong," he said, flinging the mail onto the table. "Traffic around here sucks, taxes are ridiculous and you would think I could get a decent cup of coffee for less than four bucks."

She cocked her head. "Yeah, but what's wrong?"

"You can never get a parking space and people are just so damn rude…"

"Dad!"

He stopped.

Gracie made sure he was quiet before speaking. "What's wrong?"

Stan blew out air and ran his hand through his hair. "What's-her-face made me look like a fool again tonight."

"What is your fascination with her? She sounds like a monster."

"I swear I have the worst luck with women," he muttered

88

under his breath.

A shapely feminine figure, wrapped in a skimpy towel, walked out of the bathroom, her still wet hair frizzied down the back. "Gracie, do you have a hair brush I can borrow?" The towel barely covered her bottom, drawing Stan's attention to long, toned and curvy legs. So innocent looking, so...pure, she moved with the silky softness of someone cherishing a memory.

Stan's entire body locked in place, the amount of exposed skin hitting him like an inebriating toxin.

"Oh!" the woman blurted. One hand went to her chest, the other to the bottom of the towel.

"Tanya!" Stan exclaimed. "What are you doing here?"

Flushing a deep red, Tanya bolted into the bathroom and slammed the door. They heard the sound of whimpering, bottles clinking and things being knocked over.

Stan whirled around. "What is going on?"

"Well, you see..." Gracie started, her eyes flicking left, then right. "It's like this. Tanya's hot water went out, so she asked if she could use our shower. I figured you were gonna be late again, chasing what's-her-face, so I said it would be okay. Did I do something wrong? She is our neighbor and she helps me with my homework and she makes me dinner all the time and helps me pick out clothes and seems to understand all about my boy problems and when Patti and I are fighting, Tanya knows just what I should do to make it right and she showed me how to make my internet site private so weirdos can't get me and—"

Stan held up his hands. "Gracie!"

"What?"

"Without the seven basic ballet movements. Please."

Gracie paused to appraise her father. An impish smile spread across her adorable face. Taking her time, she chose her phrasing carefully. The words came out measured. "Tanya needed help, Dad."

He looked at her with tired eyes. They were not the words of a smart-mouthed teenager, but rather those of a maturing young lady. He deflated. "Okay." Treading cautiously to the bathroom door, he leaned close. "Tanya?"

"Stan, I'm so embarrassed," she said. "I'll be gone in two seconds, I swear. Please don't be angry with Gracie, she was just being kind."

"It's all right. Hang on a minute." He sped down the hall and retrieved a thick robe from his closet. "I'm sorry I made you feel uncomfortable. Please. Take all the time you need." Turning the knob, he reached in blindly and offered the robe.

He heard bare feet. Then a soft hand on his. The touch was tender, almost caressing.

"Thank you," she whispered. The robe left his hand.

Stan pulled the door shut, went to his room and changed into jeans and a flannel shirt. When he returned, he did a double-take toward the door. Tanya, dressed in nice slacks and a tight sweater, was just leaving. She looked over her shoulder with unsure eyes, then waved nervously. A tremor rippled through his heart. Gracie's subtle cough stirred him from staring.

"She okay?" he asked.

"Yeah, a little embarrassed."

"Did she change her hair or something?"

"No."

The wrinkles in Stan's forehead crinkled. "New outfit?"

"You're just not used to seeing her out of her bag-lady motif."

"She sure looked...different."

"Yeah?"

"Yeah. I don't remember her legs being that—" He paused noticing Gracie's eyebrows nearing the ceiling. "Long."

"I guess high top sneakers qualify as flats," Gracie said, a wry smile spreading across her face.

Stan placed a fatherly hand on her shoulder. "Sorry about the way I acted."

"It's okay, you had a bad day." She shuffled her feet. "Hey, Dad? You had dinner yet?"

"Nope, I went right to Fitzy's from work."

Gracie perked up. "How do you feel about inviting Tanya over for dinner?"

"You want me to make nicey-nice."

"Noooo. She's a better cook than you are."

He smirked.

She smiled back. "But nicey-nice wouldn't be a bad idea."

***

"More meat, Stan?" Tanya asked, placing the plate of thinly carved steak near his hand, careful not to singe her arm on the long-flamed candles.

"You bet," he replied with gusto, stabbing several pieces. "You're an awesome cook, Tanya. London Broil is my favorite." He took a sip of red wine. "And I haven't had Cabernet since before Rebecca—" he stopped and swirled the liquid. Looking down, he cleared his throat. "Sorry."

"It's okay," Tanya replied. "So you like the wine?"

"How'd you know I like Italian vintage? Most people automatically go for Napa Valley."

"Oh, lucky guess," Tanya said, winking slyly at Gracie. "How's the child molester case coming?"

"Ha! Didn't I tell you? We nailed the guy."

"Really?" Tanya said. "How?"

"There's this woman that's always in Fitzy's—"

"Dad affectionately calls her 'what's her face'," Gracie interjected.

"Respectfully, of course," Tanya added.

"Hey," Stan said. "Who's milking this cow?" He thumbed his chest. "This is my story." He hesitated as both Tanya and Gracie buttoned down their faces, but the dimples broke through anyway. "Okay, so I slipped a note under Chester's door saying the woman in the blue dress at Fitzy's had photographs that proved he was sexually abusing his stepdaughter. I knew he wouldn't be able to resist her and I was right. One night he slithered into the bar looking to buy the photos off her."

"Like he's pretty sure they exist," Tanya said.

"Exactly," Stan said.

"You mean you really had photos of him?" Gracie asked. "Ewe, that's gross."

"No. They were autographed pictures of what's her face. I had Fitzy feed her some song and dance that Chester was this movie producer coming in to talk to her about including her in his next movie." When Tanya and Gracie eyed each other, he added. "She's not too bright."

"Really?" Tanya said under a withering look. "So what happened?"

"Chester went berserk, that's what happened. Knew he was being set up. Started hollering and busting up the joint. Fitzy called the cops and had the guy locked up."

"That's it?" Gracie asked.

"Muwa ha ha ha, no, that's not all," Stan said. "Enter yours truly. I worked it out with the cops to plant me in the cell before they tossed him in."

"Didn't he recognize you?"

"Amazing what a baseball hat, tank top, fake tattoo and not shaving can do to change one's appearance."

"So he thought you were a criminal," Tanya said.

"Right. I got him talking. Told him if he said he was sorry for the sexual abuse, they would go easy on him for the charge of drunk and disorderly."

Gracie set her glass down. "And he fell for it?"

"Yup." Stan scooped a deep spoonful of stuffing. "Hook, line and sphincter."

"But it's not legal," Tanya said. "You were the prosecuting

attorney."

"Nuh-uh. I removed myself from the case and gave it to another lawyer. There's no law against convicts giving each other legal advice is there?"

"Dad, you're a genius!" Gracie gushed, holding up her palm. "But watch the grunting."

"Don't mess with the best, or you lay with the rest," Stan said, returning his daughter's high five. "And I'm lifting the ban on all nuh-uh-ing tonight, Gracie. Your old man's celebrating."

"Another one bites the dust," Tanya said, a lopsided smile on her face. "Very clever, Stan. You *are* the best." She reached for Gracie's plate. "Are you finished, sweetheart?"

"I'm full," Gracie said. "Mashed potatoes and gravy are my favorite. What is that secret spice you add?"

"Onion salt. Gives it that little zing." She cast a glance over at Stan as he took another sip of wine. Quickly, she turned her head toward Gracie and flared her eyes.

Gracie nodded subtly. "Speaking of zing," she said, "do you like Tanya's new look, Dad?"

Stan put his glass down and appraised Tanya. A floral wrap with royal blue designs matching the color of her eyes and blouse draped her upper body. Her hair, pulled away from her face in a jumbled pile, sprouted in random spots as if it would cascade away at any moment. No longer having to fight his way through her bangs, he noticed how smooth her skin was: not tan, but rather a healthy shade of peach, as if freshly scrubbed. The absence of make-up detracted nothing; if anything, it drew his gaze even more to her features. The delicate nose, the soft eyes, the dark eyebrows and the gentle curve of cheekbones all worked in concert to form the second prettiest face he had ever seen. He tried to form the word "wow" but his brain would only agree to send a signal to gape his mouth.

A wavy scar at the edge of Tanya's mouth disappeared into lips that now pouted into a knowing smile. Cinching the wrap at her breastbone, she leaned forward slightly and pushed her chair back. "I'll get us more wine."

Stan's eyes widened as they followed her out of the room. He'd gotten used to seeing Tanya wearing those unflattering oversized pants with the million pockets. The change to a knee-length skirt was an exhilaration. It fit her form and the modest heels gave her just the right amount of pitch. He didn't miss any of it.

"You look great, Tanya," he said, suddenly feeling the temperature rise. "Blue works for you. Really brings out your eyes. You should dress like that all the time."

"Thanks, Stan. I'd like that."

Gracie smiled as Stan screwed up his face.

"Hey, Dad. I just got an idea. You know how you've been wanting to go out with what's-her-face, but you need to get better at dancing?"

"Gracie," he whispered, putting a finger to his lips, "we shouldn't talk about what's-her-face in front of Tanya."

"I don't mind," Tanya said from somewhere in the kitchen.

Stan flushed a bit. "Sorry, Tanya."

"It's okay. What's this obsession like?"

"From what I've been able to get out of him," Gracie said, "she's great looking, but won't have anything to do with any guy unless he is a good dancer. So Dad thinks he needs to take lessons."

"Good idea," Tanya said. "How long have you been going to class?"

Stan shifted in his seat.

She peeked around the corner. "You haven't started yet, have you?"

He shook his head.

"Maybe if you had a partner," Tanya said.

"Yeah, Dad," Gracie said, "That's a great idea. If I went

with you, you'd learn in no time."

Stan put up his hands. "I'm not taking dance lessons with a bunch of girls."

"Oh, right!" Gracie said, smacking herself in the head. "That would be, like, *totally* geeky."

"Yeah...*totally*."

Tanya's sleek figure flowed through the open doorway. "What about taking them with a woman?"

"Who am I..." Stan's voice trailed off as she shed the floral wrap to fully reveal the blue blouse buttoned at just the right depth. "...going to get..." She unfurled her hair. "...to dance..." Her blue eyes smoldered under dark eyebrows. "...with me?" A morsel of food fell off his fork.

"Why Stan," Tanya purred, "I thought you'd never ask."

"Way to go Dad!" Gracie cheered, throwing her arms around her father's neck.

As Stan led Tanya in a slow dance around the kitchen, Gracie caught her eye over his shoulder. Gracie's thumbs-up brought a man-killer smile to Tanya's face.

Note: An excerpt from *Gracie's Web* appears in *The Foiled Knight*, John's second novel. This is the first publication of the entire story.

# After School

## By: Lorraine Gilmore

Betsy never liked to hear the ringing of the school bell which marked the end of the day. Her math workbook was open, and she sat staring at it. Mrs. Rogers was doing paperwork at her desk and hadn't yet noticed that a student remained in her fifth-grade classroom. All of the children liked her except for Dylan Jones and he didn't like anybody. She never raised her voice and if someone gave a wrong answer, she never called them stupid. She would say things like "Let's read through that again and put on our thinking caps. I know you can work this out if you give it some thought."

The school was so quiet that Betsy could hear the tick tock of the clock on Mrs. Rogers' desk. She held her pencil in her hand as if she was thinking about the problems in the book instead of the ones at home. She was so filled with dread that her tummy was knotting up and she was so lost in thought that she did not hear Mrs. Rogers come up to her desk.

"Betsy, didn't you hear the school bell?"

"Oh, Hi Mrs. Rogers. I've been trying to work on some of

my homework. Our house is so noisy that it's hard for me to study at home."

That wasn't really the truth, but Betsy often lied to hide the truths about what went on behind closed doors in her home.

"I'm sorry that I can't let you stay longer. I need to leave for an appointment and it's time for me to close the classroom."

"That's O.K. Mrs. Rogers." Betsy lifted the top of her desk and took out the rest of her books. As usual, she was wearing a dress that was less than fresh and clean, and it had been poorly mended on the shoulder.

Betsy left her schoolbooks on her desk and walked over to where her coat was hanging from the peg on the wall. As she slowly put it on, she said "Thanks, Mrs. Rogers. I'll see you tomorrow."

She got her books and shuffled across the room to the door. When she got to the front steps of the school, she took a deep breath, but was unable to square her shoulders. That would take way too much effort. As she walked away, she did not notice the bright sun and the birds singing in the trees.

About a block away from the school, she took a left turn and headed over to the church graveyard. With its many trees and flowers, it was a pleasant place to drag out the length of her walk home.

This afternoon she stopped beside her favorite tombstone. It was not very big and had an angel lying across he top. She read out loud: "Eleanor Rose Garamond, 1932 – 1938, Beloved Daughter."

Was she really beloved or did they put it there to hide the truth? And, why did she die so young? Did somebody hurt her? These questions about the little girl bothered her.

"Well, if things were bad at home, at least she could be happy now with the angels up in heaven." She spoke this thought out loud and it made her feel less troubled about Eleanor.

She left the cemetery and began to walk a little faster. It wouldn't do for her to arrive home after dark or too late to clean off the kitchen table for supper.

As she walked up the front steps, she noticed that the morning paper was still lying on the front porch. This was not a good sign.

She quietly opened the front door and peeked around the corner. The house was quiet and no one was in sight. There were no pleasant smells coming from the kitchen stove. Her mom's shoes were on the floor in front of the sofa and her coat was tossed on a chair. It was not an unfamiliar sight and she knew where to go next.

Holding her breath, she moved silently down the hall to the bedroom. She peeked through the open door and saw her mom sprawled across the bed. She wrinkled her nose as the smell of stale gin wafted across the room.

"Well, at least she made it to the bed before she passed out." She said to herself.

Betsy went to the kitchen and got the cereal, a bowl and spoon from the cupboard and the milk from the refrigerator. Another night without a hot meal, but she was not disappointed. She was in the middle of reading "A Little House on the Prairie". She could read, and have a quiet meal pretending that the happy family was hers.

# Every Wednesday Afternoon

## By: Suzy Tenenbaum

It was their time together
Every Wednesday afternoon.

Hand in hand they went into the library
Pushing open the heavy wooden door.

"Pick out five books," Mommy always said
Suzy had just learned to count.

Little Suzy took her time
Touching the faces on the covers.

Petting the pages of animal books
Her eyes open wide at the picture of Bambi's mom.

She was left alone in the children's section
While Mommy went to pick out cookbooks and magazines.

Suzy didn't mind, since she was surrounded
By her friends Dr. Seuss and Winnie the Pooh.

The checkout line was short and Mommy gave her card
Suzy looked over the high counter and gave a shy smile.

They stopped at the playground on the way home
But Suzy didn't want to stay long.

Because when they arrived home Mommy read the new books
And little Suzy sat upon her lap on the worn blue couch.

After all, it was their time together
Every Wednesday afternoon.

# Harsh Realities

## By: Barbara Dullaghan

Have you ever thought that what you envisioned as true was actually just your wistful imagination? When I was young, my family spent a great deal of time with my father's family. I grew up an only child and always looked forward to the busyness of my grandmother's house. As the first granddaughter, I enjoyed lots of attention from my young teenage aunts. We would sing and dance on the front porch, away from the chaos and clutter of the railroad rooms of the apartment and its hot kitchen as Grandma prepared dinner for a virtual army. I remember that on Thanksgiving, one turkey would come out of the oven as another went in to feed the second wave of visitors.

My whole concept of family was forged at Grandma's house. Loud raucous laughter and occasional shouting were startling opposites from my relatively quiet home of just three and our family dog. Over the years, my extended family grew from eighteen aunts and uncles to well over 50 first cousins, some of whom I have never met.

I also never met my mother's parents. As a child, I did meet her brothers and sisters and we spent every Christmas Eve with my Aunt Mickie and her family. But when I was ten, I asked my mother about her parents and she told me she had been a foster child.

"Mom, what happened to your mother?" I asked. "Why didn't you live with her?"

"Well," my mother answered slowly. "It was complicated."

"What was complicated?"

"Life," she answered, looking away.

I had many more questions that would have to wait. And so my imagination created different scenarios like terrible people had pulled her out of her mother's arms and kidnapped her. It was easy for my mind to go to horrific places because the alternative of my mother not being wanted was unthinkable. And, I was very confused about her brothers and sisters. But the scenario I convinced myself to be true was that she had been loved so much by a family who found her when she wandered off, that she lived happily ever after.

Decades passed and I formed my own family of a husband and three children. Only later in my thirties did my mother begin to open up to me about her experience. I felt devastated for her when she told me that she had been abandoned at eighteen months old on a street corner in the Bronx. She was brought to an orphanage where she lived until being put into the foster care system at around ten years old.

Unfortunately, my mother had an unhappy and often abusive foster care experience. One of her brothers was at the same orphanage; they discovered each other there. I remember listening closely as she told me the story.

"One day," she started, "when I was about four, the nuns were marching us in a line to go upstairs to dinner. The boys line was going down the stairs and a little boy stopped on the stairs next to me. I remember hearing one of the nuns say, 'Oh, my, they are almost identical.' Of course, I had no idea what that meant, but the next day I was introduced to my older brother." She let out a deep sigh. "When I left the foster system at 16, I met my sister Mickie and my other brothers. They were raised by my mother."

It was then that I realized my mother hadn't been loved and didn't live happily ever after, even though she married a kind man who she prayed would never raise his hand to her or their children. He didn't. I was able to finally put some pieces together: her suicide attempts, her addictive personality, and her constant anxieties and fretful worrying. Haunted by her past, my mother struggled her whole life to cope and accept the realities that formed her life and the person she would eventually become.

Despite all of that, she was a protective mother who lived through the deaths of two premature baby sons and numerous miscarriages. She was a prolific reader and a life-long learner who earned her college degree in Nursing at age 44. As each of my three children were born, my mother thanked me for giving her another person to love. We made sure that we celebrated every Christmas Eve and morning with her because she had never had that as a child. She was an adoring grandmother who left my children with many happy memories that still make us laugh out loud. But nothing ever seemed enough to calm her inner fears that everything could disappear in an instant.

Those stories were harsh realities for me, an only child, who was loved and encouraged beyond reason by my parents and extended families. But this only child also grew up understanding empathy for other people, hard work, and the importance of resilience because of my mother's presence in my life.

# Naming Things

## By: John Stickney

The most unsung person in the history is the person who
named things what they are named now. I realize that through
the ages that has not been the exact same person. I mean, I
know whoever decided to call a rock a rock is probably not the
same person as the one who decided to call a CPU, whatever
that is, a CPU. Whoever decided that milk was milk probably
did not determine that a sump pump was a pump that sumped.
I say probably because in a world where Richard Nixon, Cher
and Bill Clinton keep coming back, despite seemingly
insurmountable obstacles like death, dearth of talent, and
political suicide, anything is possible. More likely than being
the same guy or gal, it was a person inhabited by the same
spirit, by the same innate sense of the true nature of things.
You've heard, no doubt, of the Hero with a Thousand Faces?
Of the Universal Soldier? Well, there is a universal namer out
there.

One thing I know for certain, it's not me. If this job had
been left up to me, everything in the world would be a whozit,

a thingamagig, a whatnot, a thingy. Hey, it would go, and me that whatnot, the one right next to the thingamagig. Which thingamajig? You know thingy number 157. Yeah, in the world that I named, milk would be that liquid white stuff, rocks would be those hard things that hurt when you drop them on your feet, and a car battery would be that whozit that powers the whatnot and hurts you when you drop it on your foot. My dictionary would be a enormous. Everything would have some bland label like whozit followed by a number and an alphabetical letter next to it. Huge rivers of special designations. My dictionary, my world, you would read like the IRS code.

Why is this? I'm not sure. My dad, a navigator/bombardier flying in a B17 during WWII, became a metallurgical engineer and had taught other engineers in college before switching to the private sector. He knew what things were called. Heck, he's one of the guys who named things.

My brother started off like I did, lost in the world of objects. At some point that changed. While he became a namer, my only change was to lose a little of my hay-fever. While he took to tools and gears, for some reason I didn't sneeze quite as hard as before. We were close in age, went to the same high school and college and often worked in the same places. Together, we would pool our money and buy a car. I liked to go places, he liked to work on the cars. I would try to help, sincerely try, on more than one occasion to learn something about this foreign world beneath the hood. Five minutes into each and every lesson, trying to loosen some whatnot with that thingamajig something would slip and he would skin his knuckles. Letting loose a stream of obscenities, he would then hammer the part with the thingamajig, exacting a terrible metallic revenge. Surprisingly sometimes this method worked, whatever needed to be loosened would become loose. Not always, sometimes something else would have to be beaten.

Overall, this repair method was probably close to 75% effective. But there were exceptions. For example, one time he worked on the transmission. Shortly thereafter I was proceeding south on interstate 71, our car shifted from 60 mph to neutral and before I could get it to the side of the road, shifted into reverse. It was as if the car was possessed. Once on the side of the road, it decided to move in a forward direction in what was probably second gear. I rode the berm to nearest exit. When I finally got to a pay phone and got a hold of him, it was my turn to use the one thing I did learn about cars from him, that long stream of obscenities. Today, he is the head of the maintenance department for a large, multimillion dollar factory. He knows the names of things and is probably on his way to naming a few things himself. I am certain that his vehicles only go in the desired direction.

And me? I am still lost in the world of things named by someone else, hoping that gene therapy will identify the thingy my whatnot is still missing, hoping that a gene splice, a transplant or at least a prosthetic device will eventually serve as a beacon to lead me from the darkening, whozit filled wilderness.

# Fork in the Road

## By: Terry L. Dismore

I wake to a familiar heaviness pressing into my lungs, sucking the life out of me. I acknowledge the scars being peeled very slow at first and then quick and continuous hitting with lightning-bolt intensity. My eyes start to well up and then pour a lifetime stream of salty fluids and hidden emotions. These tears have never been enough to cleanse or purge the undetected stains that hang thick, dark, looming clouds within my head. A pounding and pelting migraine seems more vigorous than in previous years.

Today, the symptoms show up accompanied by massive boulders surrounding my chest-cavity. I can only see small, hollow shadows of light in a distance. How do I escape through those narrow openings? Today is the anniversary, and a reminder of layered painful memories.

I'm at the same juncture, the same day and time, in the road seeking answers. Do I go north, south, east, or west, as if the change in direction makes a difference? Will today be different from the past thirty-six years I've tried to face my fears, or should I just retreat with a promise to meet the grief next year?

Doesn't the universe know I can't make any decisions about which way to go or what to do or even what to say? So why have I been chosen to settle this gut-wrenching life issue today of all days? I beg for mercy and forgiveness to no avail.

The anniversary of two lost lives has haunted me each year, releasing agonizing thoughts, disabling me from speaking. I retreat back to bed, pull the covers over my head, and decide to wake when the day is over. Today, I won't shower, dress, eat, drink, think, or talk to anyone. I'll stay in formatted misery mode logistically mapped out just for today.

My thoughts find me hiding under the covers when suddenly, I feel a coldness riding in on a thin, wavy vapor, invading my nostrils and, my skin making its way into my body. Well, that's just perfect: *cold on the inside to match the freezing on the outside.* I pull the covers tighter, trying to have some control over this hollow emptiness, but yet again, I fail. I'll just accept whatever today brings; after-all, I deserve it.

My heart starts to bleed tiny droplets of red liquid very slowly, which is more painful. I cry out to whoever is listening. "Who are you to make me think of this today; why can't you leave me in my misery and pain?" *Do I dare think of what today represents?* "Are you satisfied that I've died a thousand deaths? Go ahead, do your best to make today worse." I feel nothing inside. Attacked with thoughts of loss and grief, I accept my punishment.

I've been at this juncture in the road over and over again and can't seem to break through. I plead with the universe to allow my mind to drift back in time when I was better, things were better, and I knew what to do. How do I gain fierce determination over this obstacle and allow myself to return to a life worth living?

Exhausted and weary, sleep overtakes my tired body. I dream of my young self, dancing and giggling like a school-girl, happy in my own skin. Saturday nights at my house were the best. My mother is starting her marathon washing of five girls' hair. We set each other's hair with brown paper bags, duplicating the latest styles from the girly magazines. I remember the prom dress my mother purchased from thrift stores, equaling any first-class fashionista. I was the envy of all the other little girls.

Going to bed at Christmas was a special event at our house. We woke to the aroma of chicken roasting in the oven, macaroni, and cheese, sweet potatoes, collard greens and peppermints inserted into oranges for a beverage. Our tree twinkled with what seemed like a million lights and ornamental love. Thank you, Mom, for those memories and acts of kindness. *That was then, and this is now.*

Peace escapes me even in my sleep. Dreams and memories are all significant; unfortunately, the reality is real. I turn on my right side, searching and yearning for truth and assurance to return when I wake tomorrow. I just have to escape this wretched day.

I acknowledged this situation before and struggled to become whole and not this fearful person I've become. I would give anything to return to the days when I was able to gather inner strength and could crush boulders into tiny pieces of rock like a warrior princess. Where is my inner light?

Do I possess the courage to make a long distance plea for help? Once the call is activated, there is no turning back. Calling the "Elder Counsel of the Seeing-Eye Mothers" is a severe offense, punished by withdrawal from the council. I'm next in line to receive my eye mark. My tortured soul stands before the fork in the road yelling, "I must stop this torture, and evoke the counsel!"

*I, T. L. Dismore, summon my ancestral counsel past and present to come through the walls, under the blankets, into my heart, mind, and soul today.* I call seven times and wait for what seems like an eternity. Not even the elders respond or care.

I retreat into myself, wrapping the covers more tightly to calm my shivering, cold, exhausted body. I remind myself that this is an extreme measure that warrants their presence. Oh, my God, have the ancestors heard and answered my plea? I feel alone and afraid under the covers.

*I cry out; I can't breathe; I had to ask you all to come.* The bile of intimidation creeps up into my mouth, knowing full well the seriousness of the elders to grace me with their appearance could be doom for me. Am I dreaming or am I awake?

*They are here.* I acknowledge the presence of the seeing-eye mothers, prayer warriors, village historians (Griots) entering the room. I promptly get into position with my legs crisscrossed, hands in prayer, and head bowed. I attempt to explain how the boulders layered themselves around my body with heavy burdened weights pressing on my chest until I couldn't breathe. My explanation fails to calm my nerves as the elders all stand. As I start another futile attempt to speak, five hands raise in unison to silence any further comments. I yield to silence and obedience as directed by the Elder Counsel of the Seeing-Eye Mothers. They stand before me with strength etched into their skin, silver hair, arms linked in unity.

Bold.

Fearless.

The elders brought warm blankets and, carefully brewed concoctions for the ceremonial cleansing and uplifting. My mother, Julia K. Jones, and my four aunts lead the family council of elders. My Aunt Mae, ninety-one years old, isn't allowed to speak since she is our living council member. They are in a single file according to chronological age, but I soon realize they are in order by their deaths.

They are dressed in long purple flowing ceremonial robes, heads covered, signaling respect and authority. The elders have removed their sandals before stepping into a circle where I am seated. My family elders are smiling, and reassuring, with loving looks of kindness as they place all the objects evenly spaced around me. They chose purple robes, my birthstone color, representing royalty, nobility, strength, creativity, peace, devotion, pride, and beauty.

The ceremony begins with us all linking arms, in prayer, and ritual chanting. My mother covers my head with a beautiful purple headpiece, with embossed patterns that trace my ancestral tree. The songs require a call from my elders and a response from me. The family elders place their seeing-eyes in the middle of their foreheads to see and hear my pleas without outwardly speaking to preserve privacy.

The ceremony continues with the elders breaking hands to anoint my head with myrrh and frankincense. The harvesting of frankincense and myrrh is putting the villagers at risk of dying out, threatening their livelihood. These tree saps found in Africa and other countries requires responsibility and honor for ritual sacrifice. I nod in understanding and agreement for the trees and villagers that continue this tradition for sacred ceremonies.

We begin to enter the path of my life's turning point with hope for a successful outcome. The dancing and hand-holding immediately stop, but the anointing and prayers continue.

The four aunts sit and place their right hands strategically around my body. Aunt Tea anoints me to be fearless, guilt-free, and stress-free when faced with adversity. Aunt Mildred anoints me to remove all doubt, discouragement, and anger. Aunt Louise anoints and reminds me that burdens are heavy, tiring, and exhausting if allowed to continue. Now it's my mother's turn to speak. Using her eye, she sits on the floor in front of me.

"Daughter, take my hand and let's journey back to a time when we both cherished each other as mother and daughter. I was able to comfort, love and care for you in the ways of a mother to a child, but today, you're grown up and stand as an adult before me and not as a child. You have control and power over your thoughts, which govern you and your family. We, the family elders, are here to support and guide you through your continued journey until you join us.

"I know this seems a cruel phase for you to face. Losing two daughters to the afterlife before they had a start in life was tragic and devastating. However, your pain gives you the courage and drive to motivate and encourage others. You no longer need to wear the mask of shame cradled as a shroud hanging over your head. Take my hand, and crawl out of the emptiness of the past and into the lighted future where you belong.

"You aren't exempt from pain or problems. But we have planted and fortified you with sacrificial fibers of resilience planted by your family elders in your DNA. The pain you feel today must end so that you can go on and take your rightful place as a future elder, and a seeing-eye mother, not only for your daughters, but all daughters. Remember the rainbow after the rain, bright bold sunshine warm and robust, and trees that suffer ritual slaughter for you. The villagers accept their sacrifice for you to fulfill your destiny. My dear T. L. their sacrifice can't go unanswered by you.

"Go back, my daughter, to being in love with life. My darling, much has been placed on your shoulders, which is why you feel the massive boulders closing in on all sides and see only slivers of light in the distance. The flow of life requires balance and forgiveness to survive. When you were eight years old, the trumpets sounded the call, and you answered and accepted. It was then that the seeing eye was injected into your very soul and continues to grow each day. Many are called, but very few are chosen. To whom much is given, much is required. You and your sisters have been my crowning pride and joy, but you my daughter have additional responsibilities. I appreciate the love and care you gave me during my hard times and illness. We shared an extraordinary bond that only you and I understand.

"The blankets you've been hiding under are merely fluffy clouds that life has made heavy. I, your mother, and your aunts, must leave you with our family lineage that blazed a path before you with love, compassion, and kindness. Your Aunt Mae's seeing eye is still working at age ninety-one; take advantage and be strengthened and comforted by her words while she lives.

"The forks in the road are a reminder of growth and development. Obstacles force decisions to move forward or stand still; nevertheless, the choice is yours to make. If you continue to run, the challenges will continue to chase you. Stand flat-footed, and remove one boulder at a time. Look to your seeing eye that grows powerful each day, allowing you to move toward your future. We have enjoyed our visit with you, but must return to take care of the others. I'm always in your dreams and heart.

Remember to place one hand over your heart and the other over your head, and you will find us championing you. When you are ready to face the obstacles, we will be with you in numbers, and you will find strength and courage.

"Awake, daughter, to fulfill your destiny, and speak nothing of our visit. Drink plenty of water for internal cleansing of the body; bathe and go into the sunshine. Walk around and we'll shatter the boulders into little pieces with our combined energy and strength. We are with you."

My aunts step outside of the circle and leave as quickly as they came. My mother looks back as I bow, placing one hand over my heart and the other over my head. As she reminded me, it's where she will always be with me.

I wake up with a ray of hope. No one knows what tomorrow will bring, but today, I feel my soul surrender.

Asante Sana elders.

Asante Sana mother.

Until we meet again.

# An Unexpected Journey

## By: Barbara Dullaghan

The single pearl earring
in search of a match,
the high school ring
still unworn after five decades.

A promise ring of 50 years ago
tarnished, holding memories of
a love who died too soon.

A bracelet of colored sailboats
my sweet Aunt Irene,
English war bride,
bidding "Cheerio"
after a "cuppa" tea with milk and
ham sandwiches on white bread,
always with butter.

Silly, inexpensive earrings

little decorated trees or shiny bells
worn by Mom every Christmas Day
to make us smile and giggle.

Cleaning my jewelry box.
Things once forgotten
flooding my mind.

# Up, Down and All Around

## By: Suzy Tenenbaum

Up, down and all around
Spinning on the merry go round.

Hair is flying, hold on tight
First spin left, and then spin right.

Dizzy, dizzy, in a tizzy
Wait, it's not so fun.

Ashes, ashes, we all fall down
No longer smiling, now a frown.

Child's play is really work
And parenting's a dream.

Then you wake up, upside down
It isn't as it seems.

# Nothing Is Simple Anymore

## By: Diane Pascoe

I had a big problem. I was unemployed, and no longer had that company-paid life insurance that made me so attractive to my family, inheritors of my company benefits, when they envisioned me six feet under.

Although I didn't want them dancing in joy on the fresh earth above me when I passed, I wanted to be sure there was enough money for my wine and cheese wake, where everyone would be telling tall tales about me, saying "Wasn't she smart or funny, or isn't that bright red casket monogrammed with DJP so very unusual, but so very her?"

I also pictured some chocolate caramel truffles, pomegranate martinis and a little quartet churning out tunes by Otis Redding or The Temptations from my teen years. Too bad I wouldn't be there to enjoy the party.

The vision in my head of that rollicking event had distracted me from finding a new life insurance policy, and like everything I did, it was not simple. One task always led to five more.

As I started my Internet search for life insurance, an advertisement popped up saying "Life Insurance at Great Rates." I completed the on-line form and waited for my "great rates" to be emailed to me.

An hour later the phone rang. It was a sales rep, Miss Nosey, from the Great Rates Insurance Company, asking if my husband also needed insurance.

"Sure, the more the merrier," I responded. She then asked some questions about our medical histories and medications. I responded that Honey took blood pressure pills.

"Ooh," she exclaimed.

I asked her if taking these pills would be a terrible thing for insurance.

"Oh no, he should certainly take them if he needs them," she said, "even if that does change his category."

*Category?* Talk of categories sounded expensive—I braced myself for the questions that I knew were coming.

"How tall is your husband and what does he weigh?" she asked.

"Six-foot-two and I don't know his weight," I lied. The tall tales had begun.

Then she hit the mother lode. "How tall are you and what do you weigh?"

I replied that I was 5'5" and fat. *That's the bottom line, Miss Nosey. Skip the actual weight.*

She threw out a number, as though she were guessing weights at the fall fair.

"Nope, way fatter," I proclaimed. I could have told her my real weight, but my coyness was amusing me.

She tried again with a bigger number.

"Nope, fatter."

"Oooh!" she said.

It was at that point I realized that "oooh" was her way of calculating her commission, which escalated with our weights.

She decided to try a new approach. She asked if my weight fell within a certain range.

"Yes, it does," I heard myself saying, as my Pinocchio nose grew. I reasoned that I would be in that weight range by the time I met my maker, so it wasn't exactly lying.

"I don't have any more questions," said Miss Nosey.

I breathed a sigh of relief, but the bliss was temporary.

"So what date would be good for Mr. Walker to come to weigh and measure you?"

The other shoe had finally dropped! Why didn't she tell me about the home visit before I misrepresented everything about myself? And how would I explain to Mr. Walker my sudden twenty-pound increase over the weight range that Miss Nosey had recorded. Do I tell him it is water retention? Constipation?

Exhausted, I told Miss Nosey I would need to talk to Honey about when we could see Mr. Walker, and then I'd call her back . . . *maybe in a year or two,* I said under my breath. Honey and I needed to exercise big-time before we could afford to buy life insurance.

Nothing is simple anymore.

# Our Life With Mother and Father

## By: Lee Norman Mehler

I guess we were what was called "upper middle class". Growing up in Long Island seemed like a normal existence. I didn't know there were people unlike me in the world. It was the 1950's and life was simple and safe. Doors were left unlocked when you were away from home. We walked to grade school in our primarily Jewish neighborhood without chaperones. Music had rich harmonies with the seeds of raucous rock and roll in the years to come. Mom and Dad were going to be together forever. Family was here in town, or in the next town, well before the scattering of brothers, sisters, and cousins to the deep south and west coast.

Our grandparents were a constant in our lives because mother and father believed that family should be cherished. Every Wednesday I walked the seven blocks to Cameron Park Elementary School in the morning and ran the same seven blocks home because our grandparents were there. I can still smell Grandfather's sweet cigar that filled our green clad, split level home at 3 p.m. They stayed for dinner and the scent stayed for days after. Mother brought out the black paged albums of scalloped-edge polaroid photographs that were kept in place by triangular tabs at the corners. She took us on a tour of all the faces of friends and relatives both still alive and those becoming distant memories. We traveled around the globe as we gathered before the fading evidence of a world of exotic adventures extending far beyond the confines of the living room.

As we children played and marveled at the possibilities of the life to come, Mother slipped into the kitchen to magically create the dinner we had taken for granted. We sat down to the fragrant meal of pot roast, baked potato, and brown sugar glazed carrots that I still can smell today. We would sleep well that night with full stomachs and heads stuffed with new dreams of an unlimited future.

My Father and Grandfather owned an upholstery fabric mill in Paterson, New Jersey. The clanging shuttles in the giant looms would later claim the better part of my father's hearing. The 110 people who worked in the mill seemed like family who knew my younger brother, my sister and me by our first names. They were all friendly before the advent of the unions in the mill stole away the closeness of this extended family.

The corporate offices for the company were on the forty fourth floor of the Empire State Building. We visited every Thanksgiving Day and rode up the elevators taking care to choose the express elevator that would travel so fast that our ears popped. We flung open the double doors of the wood paneled office lobby to be greeted by the receptionist with the eternal smile and the foot high, beehive hairdo. We played with the newest gadgets such as the IBM Selectronic typewriter that spelled out our gibberish faster than we could think.

Between Thanksgiving and Christmas the city was magical as we walked up Fifth Avenue, hand in hand with our mother, gazing up at the competing windows in Gimbel's and Macy's, sparkling with the light dusting of snow. We stopped at every elegant display of foreign lands or childhood story books that were illustrated with moving figures of fantasy scenes meant to lure us inside to buy their wares. We rode the softly clanking wood escalators floor after floor until we reached what seemed like heaven at the top level full of toys. It was impossible to choose just one toy as directed by mother and father, but we eventually made that perfect choice.

After shopping, we walked to my Grandfather's house on Park Avenue overlooking Central Park. Our home on Long

Island was nicely appointed, but my Grandfather's house was slightly more opulent. His silverware was gold plated, or at least a good fake.

I remember the entrance to his home like it was yesterday. We spotted the gleaming chrome and glass swinging door under the green barrel vault awning from a block away. The soaring façade of the elegant apartment building was guarded by the tall, smiling doorman who knew everyone by name.

We took the elevator, accompanied by the operator, who we thought lived in this small space since he was always there whenever we visited. We burst out of the confines of the elevator and raced to the large, solid entrance to Grandfather's home. Beyond the door was a wonderland of smells and textures that still affect my soul today. The overstuffed furniture, heavy brocade curtains and exotic art were antiques in the future, but were new at that time.

There were many highlights that day including a balcony view of the Macy's Thanksgiving Day Parade passing below. There were large syncopated brass bands rumbling by. Every few minutes we could spot the next approaching giant inflated balloon held to the ground by dozens of clowns. They struggled to keep Popeye or Betty Boop, who were floating at our eye level, from releasing with each stiff wind.

The usual Thanksgiving feast was started each year by the serious discussion between my Father and Grandfather about whether the proper way to carve a turkey was sitting down or standing up. Since this was Grandfather's home and he was doing the carving, it usually was accomplished sitting down, despite the logical engineering arguments against his method.

The filling meal was crowned by the double chocolate layer cake crafted by the cook, Rosie, who could transform cocoa, butter cream and dark chocolate shavings into an eight-inch high dream. This dessert alone made Rosie an important member of the extended family.

Thanksgiving was our favorite holiday. It seemed to unite us and the country into one big family. Being full at the end of the long day helped us sleep on the long ride home as the steady hands of my father guided the '57 Buick Roadmaster east on the Long Island Expressway. Our mother, in the front seat, serenaded us as her voice accompanied the radio to the latest Rogers and Hammerstein's show tune. It was easy to sprawl out on the back-bench seat since they had not yet invented seat belts. As we passed under the street lamps they cast a rhythmic pattern of light and dark, marking our way home.

The innocence of the day would be lost soon enough as we grew into adults and had our own children to whom we could pass along our own traditions. We would hold fast to the good times that were here as the past slipped away with our childhood. We had no idea that this idyllic day was going to disappear with time and progress. All we have left are memories. But maybe that was enough.

# An Impromptu Road Trip

## By: Claudia Blanchard

We decided to visit heaven. You know, that place in the sky where the sun always shines, and the clouds are puffy and white. In a small bar in Venice after a few rounds of Aperol spritzes, my best friend Chris and I agreed it would be a fun day trip; a chance to visit briefly with family and friends we had not seen nor heard from in decades. Just a quick drop-in, a spontaneous jaunt to catch up on things. "Hi, how ya doin?", that sort of pleasant exchange.

Neither one of us was afraid or even hesitant. Chris and I relished new adventures and had traveled to many exotic places before – Antarctica, Easter Island, Mozambique. The obvious question facing us was, how do we get to heaven? We could chant, then meditate, we could sauté some magic mushrooms in this flavorful olive oil I bought in Naples. Or, we could, you know, make it a longer stay and drink the Kool-Aid, chomp on the cyanide pill.

When I thought about meeting my mother in heaven, I realized how very strange it would be. I was now nearly twice mom's age. I am the daughter with wrinkles and gray hair to her smooth skin and jet-black ponytail. She was 38 when she died, and I'm in my late sixties. I would recognize her, but would she know me? Then, I thought, how much time could I spend with her when there were many others to visit – Dad, Nana, Uncle. Oh, and Dad was cremated; his ashes scattered in the Gulf of Mexico. Would this matter? How would he appear? Would he be solid in form or an ashy ghost all glimmer and shimmery?

I might also bump into friends I didn't know were in heaven. What do you say to a dead friend you didn't know was dead? "Hey, how are you?", "Good to see you again." "Me? No, I'm not dead. Just visiting for the day." There was also the concern that I could meet up with people who didn't like me down on Earth. My ex-husband, the students I caught cheating and failed, the cop I flipped the bird!

Oy, this adventure could be more complicated than I thought. Perhaps this impromptu road trip wasn't such a great idea after all. Better to order another Aperol spritz.

# At the Show of Old Age

## By: Suzy Tenenbaum

I have a front row seat
At the show of old age.
Front and center, in a red, cracked leather seat
I sit and watch, hankie in hand.

Sometimes I look away from the show
The scene is too revealing and personal.
I have my coat over my head, but it's too late
I've already seen it.

I willingly bought a ticket to this show
And I knew the basic story,
But up close the main character is so compelling
I lean forward in my seat.

She steps to the front of the stage
And gives a soliloquy on
How there is nothing else to look forward to,
"All the good things have happened already."

Perhaps that is true for me too
Maybe very little is left.
I want to run out of the theatre,
Drive to the airport and hop a plane to Nairobi.

Then there is a funny, sweet scene
And I'm so glad I've come to the show.
Mom and I are lying on the bed together
Holding hands, hers cool and mine warm.

We are telling stories of our shared past and laughing.
That scene slows my heart rate,
Offers a bit of rest
Before the final act.

# Feed Your Face

## By: John Stipa

From a passion for food to passionate relationships, to wearing emotions on their sleeves, and talking with their hands, Italians are an expressive bunch. And nothing brings the full and robust culture together like a holiday dinner.

Christmas Eve at our house was more than just a family gathering. It qualified as an event, complete with food, wine, gifts and laughter. If NFL football had The Super Bowl and soccer The World Cup, then Italians had Christmas Eve and The Feast of the Seven Fishes.

For the un-anointed, The Seven Fishes is a meal served using seven different kinds of seafood. Christmas Eve is a vigil or fasting day, and the abundance of seafood reflects the observance of abstinence from meat until the feast of Christmas Day itself. The tradition comes from southern Italy, where it is known as *La Vigilia* (The Vigil). This celebration commemorates the wait for the midnight birth of the baby Jesus.

There may have been an official list at one time of the

proper seven types of fish to include, but since Mom ruled the kitchen, that restriction didn't apply in our house. If she was going to slave over a burning stove, she did whatever was most convenient for her. No one complained.

Christmas Eve in an Italian household starts days ahead of time with a trip to the wharf for some authentic fish just off the boat. Calamari, smelts, cod and sardines were typical selections. Notably, we never had lobster, crab, or shrimp. My guess is they were expensive fish and since Mom grew up in poverty, she went for what she remembered from her childhood as being affordable, or catchable on her own.

The fish was prepared in many ways, from breaded and fried, to baked, or sautéed in lemon butter. One unique dish was anchovies rolled into dough and deep-fried. Mom called it "freetdee". My favorite was calamari, which was slow cooked in a marinara "sugo" sauce that had been simmering for three days in a cast iron cauldron that hung from a witch's tripod.

In many Italian households, marinara sauce is called gravy. Mom didn't like calling it that since in America, gravy went on mashed potatoes. Besides, sugo sounded more exotic and smelled decadent with its garlic and rich herb spicing. The zesty flavor transported your taste buds to Florence and caused your eyes to dreamily close. Sugo was to die for and we wrestled for hunks of bread to dip so deeply that the sauce dripped down our chins and moans emanated from our throats.

Pasta, the lone side dish, took all day to prepare since it was homemade from flour, eggs and water. Occassionally, I was allowed to hand feed the dough into a manually cranked spaghetti-cutting machine. I then transferred the thousands of strands to hanging racks to dry out before boiling. Dropping a few strands of spaghetti onto the floor earned me a yank on the earlobe and eviction from the kitchen. As the aroma grew and filled the house, we passed time playing cards or talking.

Italian cards are quite different from American in that there are only forty playing cards in a deck. Hmmm, forty, another significant number in Christianity. Coincidence? I think not. Italian cards consist of four suits, three of which are the same as non-Italian card decks: clubs, spades, and diamonds. But instead of hearts, the fourth suit is cups, or maybe chalices in keeping with the religious references. What is interesting is the symbolism on the cards themselves. Clubs are depicted as pieces of wood, spades are swords and diamonds take the appearance of the sun. Italian card games (that I know of) are not as intricate as say the American Spades or Bridge and do not require bidding. Rather, most games are simple matching or pick-up in nature.

By contrast, the conversations were intricate and volatile. Politics, personal relationships, neighborhood gossip, school, work… everything was fair game since it was just family. The conversation flowed through my father, as if he were the train conductor of topics. It could go on for hours.

All the while, the smell of Italian cuisine wafted through the air causing our mouths to salivate. And therein lies a trick Mom used (I think she invented it)—she starved her family so that even if cardboard were served, we would gobble it up and claim nirvana.

The art in The Seven Fishes is in the timing of serving. Seven different dishes, each having a unique style of preparation, necessitated a skilled hand. Mom was the unequalled maestra of the gas stove. Juggling seven pans on only four burners rivaled any circus act. When one dish approached completion, the heat came down. If a dish was behind schedule, the flame height rose. Olive oil flowed, spatulas clanked, salt, pepper, garlic and oregano flew. A completed dish exited the surface to the warmth of the holding pen: the oven.

I swear that Mom could hear the collective growls of our stomachs because at just the right moment, she always announced that dinner was served. There was no dinner bell or butler to make a nasal proclamation or servers to deliver a finely timed multi-course meal. That extravagance was reserved for the rich. We were the product of poverty, so dinner arrived in calamitous fashion: simultaneously in seven different bowls with Mom uttering three words: "Feed your face."

We loved it. Could there be any better command from your mother on Christmas Eve than to dive into a feast with such unabashed gluttony? No way. I will always remember how the *baccala* (cod) melted in my mouth, the surprise of biting through an outer layer of crunchy beer-battered breadcrumbs to reach the lemon-butter tenderness of flounder. From the saltiness of smelts and sardines, to the zing of anchovy freetdees (followed by a sip of Chianti!), to the dreamy succulence of calamari and mussels in sugo sauce, no meal from any fine restaurant in the world could match Mama Stipa's Seven Fishes.

The feast became our family's most memorable Christmas present on a most special night.

# Not My Mother's Bingo

## By: Claudia Blanchard

Friday evening in the crowded downtown Chelsea hall
sitting shoulder-close on folding chairs with           .
five and more numbered sheets begging to receive the press of
colored circle stamps
bellows the baritone, Sofia
"B-21, B-21."
Tall, steroid-muscular and flamboyant, the emcee is gorgeous
and the boys in the parlor adore him
and the girls covet his sequined designer dress.

Tonight's games are sponsored by *American Express*;
sniffing high, high income levels.
Players with no progeny,
no future college educations to finance,
no dependents to siphon funds.

Sofia's jokes are at my expense
and the scattered few with like proclivities.

For most, the camaraderie of family is here among friends who love Broadway, ballet and bingo.

# Open Your Eyes

## By: Terry L. Dismore

Imagine, all we must do is open our eyes, what a novel idea. The simplicity that life offers each and every day of our lives if we just open our eyes.

Today I'm going to look through lenses without red, blue, yellow or purple to utilize my inner seeing eye for soul discovery. I'm exhilarated about the possibilities and adventures that await.

I need to pack courage and leave fear at home. I think I'd better add hope, love, and kindness; never know who I'll meet on the road that just might need a little motivational encouragement. I've decided to leave an open-heart space for the unknown soul to soul encounters from the universe.

Do you remember meeting that special someone and the unmistakable sparkle in your eyes that let you recognize "this is the one"?

The anticipation of seeing a grandchild walking through the door eyes bright, arms wide open wanting and waiting for the love hug.

The look on everyone's faces' at a good Broadway play, movie or book you can't stop thinking about. I love the view of the ocean on a bright day, trees swaying in the distance, not a cloud in the sky, a gentle misty breeze circling across your face. Do you feel the awe of it all?

Unconditional love should be served as a dose a day.

The stage is set. Lights, camera, action—you're on. What will you see today if you dare to remove your lenses?

Your (ME) Motivational Encouragement!

"Everyone walks past a thousand story ideas every day. The good writers are the ones who see five or six of them. Most people don't see any."

- Orson Scott Card

# Itchy Tights

## By: Suzy Tenenbaum

"I hate those tights. They're too itchy, Mommy. I'm not going to wear them!" Suzy screams, flinging them across the room and watching them disappear down in the space between the bed and the faded wallpaper.

Her mother sighs deeply. This was a repeat performance by her daughter and it showed in the creases of her mom's forehead. "So what do you plan to wear on this cold day? You can't walk to school with nothing on your legs!"

"I don't care! Then I won't go to school!" says the six year old.

Her mother loves the little towhead with the fly away hair and she knows the clock is ticking, so she draws another deep breath to stay calm. Without the breath, for sure she would loudly blurt out, "Get the goddamn tights on this minute, Suzanne!" But, experience has taught her that never works. Yelling at her daughter would only result in more tears and full on sobbing that nearly made her daughter throw up.

"How about wearing knee socks with the green wool

pleated skirt and the matching vest?" her mother asks in a sweet voice. "You like that one, right?"

"No, I hate that one too. It's itchy and it's a boy color. It looks like a cowboy outfit with that vest."

"Fine. Pick a dress you like, then put on your cardigan. And how about you pull up a pair of your corduroy pants, under the dress, to cover your legs? Then take off your pants as soon as you get to school, before Principal Krumbiegel sees you."

"I think that will be too bunchy," Suzy says with a pouty face. She starts to stick her tongue out, but quickly pulls it back. She glances over and sees the tights are still hidden between the wall and the bed and decides to put on the blue flowered dress and the corduroy pants; at least it's better than those itchy tights.

Now into the kitchen for round two of the Suzy wars. "What would you like for breakfast?" her mother asks calmly. "Toast and peanut butter?"

"No."

"Egg and toast?"

"Double no!"

"Rice Krispies with milk and yes, Suzanne, I know you don't like milk. How about Rice Krispies with chocolate milk?"

"Okay, but I don't like them after they get soggy," says Suzy as she gets in her chair and begins to swing her feet, not so much in joy, but rather in anxiety about the upcoming day in first grade. There the teacher will demand to see everyone's handkerchief to "see if you are prepared" and will ask the class to "raise your hand if you went to bed by seven o'clock."

Suzy could never raise her hand, because that would be lying and Suzy didn't lie. She asked her parents to please put her to bed at seven, but they never did. Daddy didn't get home until 6:00 from driving the coffee truck and then they ate dinner together. By the time Suzy and her sister had baths and read books and maybe watched "Make Room for Daddy" it was a bit past eight. Perhaps it was worth it, since, while sitting on daddy's lap and watching the TV show, he let her use her little comb and place small barrettes in his arm hairs, which made her feel like a real hairdresser.

Life was tough when your first-grade teacher made you nervous and your parents didn't let you go to bed early enough to be able to raise your hand for the "I Got Enough Sleep Club." But not wearing itchy tights and having Rice Krispies with chocolate milk for breakfast, made life a little easier.

# Another Realization

## By: John Stickney

My origin story

Involves antlers.

Oh honey,

The bar maid says,

Everyone's origin story

Involves antlers,

You are sitting midday

In a bar in Wisconsin.

It's true,

Above the bar

There's an autographed picture

Of Bart Starr next to one of Bret Farve

Next to one of Aaron Rodgers

Next to an unautographed one of Jesus

Wearing a 'cheesehead' halo.

And there's hammering Hank Aaron

Beside a team photo of the 1971 NBA Champion Bucks

Next to this year's team

And the disembodied heads

 Of actual twenty-point bucks.

Another Schlitz?

She asks.

# Where I Come From

## By: Claudia Blanchard

I come from a place where death was not discussed. Where Mrs. Levy from the dimly lit apartment next door never wore short sleeves to hide her number tattoo we all knew was there and Nana would slip into Yiddish when little pitcher with big ears was around.

I come from a place rich in aunts and uncles and a horde of cousins my age who rode bikes in sunless alleyways between city buildings. Where Bubba kept a live carp in the bathtub; her main ingredient for the Sabbath's gefilte fish.

I come from a place that drew my parents to a new place. A Levittown-type development of tiny houses built upon abandoned potato farms. A generation chasing a better life than aunts and uncles and city cousins could provide.

# Author Bios

**Claudia Blanchard** is an Emerita Professor of Marketing, Her research has been published in various academic journals. Her poems and literary criticism appear in *Eclipse* (Siena Heights University Press) and *Bridges* (Indiana University Press). She is currently writing a book of creative nonfiction.

**Terry L. Dismore** moved from New York a little over two years ago to a small town in North Carolina. Her home is surrounded by the perfect idyllic surroundings in a picturesque community bursting with nature and creativity for writing.

**Barbara Dullaghan** retired from a career in Gifted Education and is the co-author of The Smart Start Series for ages 3-5, published by Prufrock Press. She is presently working on her first novel set in her hometown of Sleepy Hollow, NY.

**Lorraine Gilmore** is originally from Mississippi and has been a Brunswick Forest Snowbird for two years. She retired from an executive placement firm about 14 years ago. She began writing essays and poetry in 1974 and **Matilde**, a picture book for children ages 3 to 8, is her only published work. She is also a member of a writing collaborative in Massachusetts where she spends the warmer months.

**Lee Norman Mehler** has lived in Brunswick Forest for two years after his 38-year residency in Durham, NC. Originally from the New York and New Jersey, he was an architect with no prior formal writing experience when he started composing fiction at the age of 66. He had written birthday poetry, wedding toasts and eulogies in his former life.

**Diane Pascoe** and husband Eric retired in Leland, NC, having lived in Raleigh and Toronto for many years. In addition to publishing essays in local publications, Diane's book "Life Isn't Perfect, but My Lipstick Is" was recently released.

**John Stickney** was born, lived and worked in Cleveland, Ohio. He and his lovely wife, and their dog Pirate, moved to Brunswick Forest in 2016. John has published poetry, fiction, nonfiction and criticism.

The Awful Truth previously appeared in performance on Cleveland's NPR Station WCPN's Morning Edition program. It is dedicated to my children and The Marx Brothers.

Naming Things previously appeared in performance on Cleveland's NPR Station WCPN's Morning Edition program. It is dedicated to my father and my brothers

The poem Paper previously appeared in the magazine Exquisite Corpse and in the poetry collection These American Moments. It was inspired by my wife, our children and the nightly question – What's for Dinner?

The poem Bless the Child previously appeared in the magazine Forum. It is dedicated to my wife and our children.

The poem Another Realization, inspired by the 'where I'm from exercise', is appearing in print for the first time. It is dedicated to my mother and father and all those ancestors and relatives back in Wisconsin.

**John Stipa** loves the beach, woodworking, playing and coaching sports, traveling, good food and storytelling. He is the author of adventure / mystery / romance novels including The Angel Solution, The Foiled Knight and No Greater Sacrifice. He has also published several short stories with his writing groups.

**Suzy Tenenbaum** retired to sunny North Carolina after living 44 years in Vermont. She loves being outside on her bike or taking long walks with her husband and dog. She is delighted to be part of the Writers of the Forest and writes memoir, essays, and poetry for children and adults.

Made in the USA
Columbia, SC
28 November 2018